Pain Seeking Understanding

In search of hope & healing

Keith C Kraft

ISBN:1727791398
ISBN-13:9781727791396

DEDICATION

In memory of Benjamin Charles Kraft.
Dedicated to my wife Debra and our children: daughter Valissa and her husband Alex and their children Myka & Bennett, son Andrew and his wife Jessica and their children Julianne & Charlotte and to all those who have lost loved ones to mental illness and suicide

The cover photo is a picture of Ben looking out on a valley in Rocky Mountain National Park in Colorado in 2009.
Photo by Keith C Kraft

CONTENTS

ACKNOWLEDGMENTS

My wife Deb for her love, support, and encouragement which has been a source of strength to help me get through these past four years. I would not have wanted to go through this process of grief with anyone else. Mobridge United Congregational United Church of Christ for their support after the death of our son Ben. Thank you for your patience with me. A special thank you to Jeri and Richard "Mitch" Behringer for their proofing, insights, and encouragement on this project. Thank you to Marilyn Schlekaway for agreeing to perform the final proofing of this project.

Forward

Reading Keith Kraft's Pain Seeking Understanding is a powerful experience. Over a period of almost four years, Keith writes his way through the pain, thoughts, and experiences of the death by suicide of his son Ben. Keith writes not only as a grieving father but also as a deeply faithful pastor.

Keith wrote each vignette or "blog" at a different part of his journey, offering different feelings, reactions, and ponderings. He writes about the shock of first knowing, the sadness of the loss of a child, the effects of severe mental illness hidden from those who loved Ben, and ways of coping with the continuing grief. He also offers help to those of us who want to support the grieving person without using platitudes.

I found it best to read the book in short periods of time and to choose passages which helped to enlighten me at different times. It is a book to carry with me for as long as I need to. Keith's journey toward understanding will help many of us on our own journey.

Peace and hope,

Jeri S. Behringer, EdD

Pastor and Counselor

CHAPTER 1

Suicide shock

(an introduction)

There are days that just run one into another in a continuous string of days. Nothing separates one day from another. Time rolls on like an ever-rolling stream. Then there are days where time just seems to stop …freeze where it is and just hangs there in midair with no suspension. Actually, it is a person's life that seems to freeze and hang without suspension. Time and the rest of the world march mercilessly on. That day was December 8, 2014 for my wife Deb and me.

The phone rang at five o-clock in the morning. It was the phone call that every parent dreads. It was a call from our youngest son Ben's sergeant in the South Dakota National Guard. He was outside our door with a police officer waiting to give a couple of parents the news that no person wants to deliver. Our son Ben had died. Not only had he died, he died from suicide. To say shock, would be an understatement. Suicide? A person knows that suicide happens …but not in my family. My whole being shattered into brokenness. My life …my wife's life …our family's life would never be the same.

This shock not only went through our family but our church family also, as well as those in our community who knew Ben. No one suspected it. No one saw it coming. The only indication that we had that Ben had any suicidal thoughts at all came when he was in high school some seven years earlier. I was sitting in the church office when I received a phone call from Ben's principal. "Mr. Kraft," the principal said, "You need to come to my office. Your son is sitting in my office and he is talking about experiencing 'dark places.' " "Dark places," then but no real serious indication since then.

The death of a loved one always brings with it its challenges. The death of a child brings its own unique challenges. The death of a loved one from suicide brings with it another set of challenges. One of those challenges is that no one knows how to take you or act around you. Some people would rather just avoid you rather than face the awkwardness that comes with suicide. Suicide makes people uncomfortable to even say, much less know how to respond to family members who have experienced it.

The curious thing with suicide is that people want to make sense of it. We need a reason for the death. Accidents, we understand. Although we wonder why, we know that accidents happen. Diseases, we know about. Natural causes make sense. We accept the reality that the body ages and organs quit working. But when a young person or a person in the prime of his or her life takes his or her own life, we just cannot wrap our mind around it. It does not make sense. We need someone or something to blame. We find it hard to accept something that does not make sense. To most of us, suicide just does not make sense. It is hard to put one's finger on mental illness or why someone would choose to end her or his own life.

Suicide victims also usually come with a certain stereotype. They were abused. They came from a broken family. Drugs or alcohol were involved. They came from poverty. There is very little hope for their future. The parents put too much pressure on them to succeed or to be a certain way. I know the stereotypes because I used to think or wonder about most of them at one time or another. The other thing with suicide is that it comes with a stigma with some people. I received a "sympathy" card from a well-meaning individual that basically said, "In spite of Ben's actions I will struggle to be proud of him."

It was at that point that I knew I had to say something. I knew that I needed to speak out, not just for my family but for all of the families who have ever lost a loved one to suicide. The attitudes and the stigma that go with suicides and mental illness have to change. I am not going to be ashamed of my son and I am not going to be ashamed of the way he died. Those who lose a loved one to suicide should never have to be ashamed of their loved one or the way that he or she died. I am proud of my son just as I am proud of my other two children. His death is not going to change that.

Ben does not fit the mold for what we think of when we think of suicide victims. Not that my family is special or anything, but I realized that if suicide could happen in my family, it could happen in any family. Mental illness does not discriminate. It is for that reason that I share my personal journey through the grief process of the loss of our son from suicide.

It is ironic really that I offer these writings in the hopes that my thoughts and personal experience might in some small way help others. It is ironic because after our son Ben's death by suicide I did not want any help. It would rather irritate me when people would suggest readings or writings that might be helpful with dealing with the death of a family member by suicide. I know the offerings were meant to be helpful and they were well-meaning. But I did not want to hear or read about dealing with death or grief. I also did not want to hear about other people's experience or their loved ones. Some of it was because I was too busy dealing with my own loss and grief and I did not want to hear about someone else's. Some of it was that I felt like people were trying to "fix" me and I did not want to be "fixed." I was going to deal with my son's death in my own way, on my own terms, and on my own time.

So it is with all humility that I offer these writings to you. I offer them, just as they are. There are no answers. There are no "fixes." There are only questions, thoughts, and ponderings that I have shared on my journey through the pain and loss of our son by suicide from a mental illness that he kept so well hidden. It is my journey of "pain seeking understanding." A journey that I am still on. A journey that will continue for the rest of my life.

It is my hope that through my journey you might find some words of comfort for your journey, whatever that journey in life might be. I also hope that through my story, it might help in some small way to continue to erase some of the stigma that goes with mental illness and suicide. My hope is that these writings might encourage you to begin thinking and pondering about mental illness and suicide in ways that maybe you had not considered before. If nothing else, I hope that these writings help to raise awareness of the reality of mental illness and suicide, and how it can happen in any family.

The following writings are blogs that I have written over the past three and two thirds of a year since Ben's death. Through reading these words, may you in some way experience some sense of…

Blessings & peace,
Pastor Keith

CHAPTER 2
THE JOURNEY BEGINS

I am Ben

I am Ben
I am of Keith and Deb, Lee and Darlene, Don and Thelma.
I am a brother of Valissa and Alex, Andrew and Jessica
I am an uncle of Julianne
I am the best friend of Hailey

I am the foothills of Wessington Springs,
the river breaks of the Missouri
I am a child of Eden Seminary, and Mobridge Schools.
I am a young man of Northern State University
and Augustana University.
I am the farm. I am the city. I am the small town.

I am a warrior of the South Dakota National Guard
I am the 200th, a proud builder of bridges;
I am a veteran of Afghanistan.
I am theater, Northern Fort Players and Black Hills Playhouse

I am music, drama and speech
I am an advocate for the voiceless.
I am a hunter …a lover of the outdoors

I am joy and happiness. I am pain and depression
I am the person you see.
    I am the person I keep hidden deep inside.
I am confident. I am uncertain
I am hope for the future. I am despair for today.

I am a child of the church
I am a person of faith.
I am loved by God and by many.
I am Ben.

As seen by Keith and Deb Kraft
December 12, 2014

December 13, 2014

Letter at Ben's funeral

Dear family and friends,

Thank you for being here and for your show of love and support to our family. To my church family here in Mobridge, I know that all of you are hurting as well and I wish I could help you through this time. To all of you, please be patient with Deb and me as we muddle through this time of loss. To Deb's students, please be understanding if some time out of the blue for seemingly no reason to you that Mrs. Kraft crashes and burns in your class. To all of you, please be understanding that I am not a very good care receiver. I am much more comfortable being on the other side of this.

All of us here know that death brings with it deep pain. Suicide, (yes, I'm going to say the "s" word) suicide brings with it its own unique pain. For as long as I can remember, people have been trying to rationalize and make sense of suicide. Some want to judge. Some want to blame. I have heard that suicide is a selfish act. I have heard that suicide is a mean thing to do for those left behind. I do not have the answers.

This much I do know. Ben was not a mean person. Ben loved and enjoyed people. Ben was not a selfish person. Ben cared about everyone, but especially those whom the rest of society would probably overlook. Ben loved life. Ben loved God. Ben was a person of faith.

What I knew a little but didn't know to what extent is that Ben also had some dark places. It was not where he wanted to go, but there were times that he would be taken there. It was not who he wanted to be, but it eventually won out. If there is anyone here who has experienced those dark places for yourself, please, please seek help. Please, please tell someone you love.

I want you all to know this. Ben loved people. Ben was loved. Ben cared for people. Ben was cared for. I know he knew it here in his heart. I just don't think he quite accepted it up here in his mind. Sadly, the dark power of the mind won out over the power of the heart this time.

For me and my family and many of us gathered here, there is no joy. There is only pain and emptiness. But we must also have hope. It is only hope that can eventually move us from this pain and emptiness to a future joy. But we must have hope or there will be no joy.

CHAPTER 3
SUICIDE AND MENTAL ILLNESS

January 12, 2105

Suicide and mental illness

My son died of mental illness. Yes, my son committed suicide. Yes, he took his own life in a violent, horrible way. It is a thought and an image that haunts me and probably will the rest of my life. I am by no means an expert on mental illness or on suicide and I, in no way want to become a parent with a cause carrying around a soap box to speak from, but here are some of my thoughts based on my personal experience from this tragedy in our family. In short, suicide is the final result of an illness …mental illness.

Think about it. If someone dies of cancer, we do not say, "My mom died from all of these bad cells in her body taking over all of her good cells and killing her vital organs." No, we say, "My mom died of cancer." If a loved one dies from a heart attack, we do not say, "My dad died from his blood flow being restricted to the heart." No, we say, "My dad died of a heart attack or a medical term might be 'cardiac arrest.' "

But society does not look at mental illness and suicide in the same way as it does other illnesses. With suicides we examine the person, not the symptoms. We examine their life. We wonder, what could have been so terrible in their life that they would do such a horrific act? We analyze their past. We wonder what event in their past made them this way? We question how they were raised and those who were responsible for their upbringing. We wonder who might have possibly done or not done something to this person to make him or her act in this way.

Go ahead. Examine, analyze, and question my son's life and surroundings. I have and I have found nothing. Maybe you can find something I have overlooked. What I have found is a brilliant, caring young man with a loving, caring, supportive family with events in his life that helped to shape him in very positive ways into a mature, thoughtful, and caring adult. Perfect upbringing? No. Challenges along the way? Yes. But nothing that a person can point at to say, "That is it. That is what made my son do this terrible thing."

So we can't blame it on environmental surroundings. We can't blame in on a person or an act. We can't blame it on a horrific event. We cannot blame it on the military or his experience in Afghanistan. Then we have to conclude that it was mental illness. Even if you could blame it on environmental surroundings, a person or an act, or a past horrific event, it is still mental illness and should be treated and acknowledged as such. It should be treated and acknowledged with the same dignity and respect of any other disease.

Mental illness is not a spiritual issue. Mental illness is not a matter of a lack of faith. It is not something that can be just prayed away and fixed by prayer and faith. It is not about demons and the devil or spiritual warfare. Mental illness is a medical issue that we as a society do not understand so some have personified it as demons.

Suicide is a mean and selfish act. It leaves the family in pain and emptiness. But we have to remember that it was the act that was mean and selfish, not necessarily the person who was mean and selfish. It is the disease beyond the individual's control that created a person that most of us did not know.

Suicide is the second or third leading cause of death among teens and young adults. But we also know that suicide can happen at any age. Mental illness can happen in any family, even those who experienced loving, supportive families.

My son died from mental illness. Hopefully, someday they will find a cause and a cure so other people will not have to experience the same pain as our family and many others have experienced.

CHAPTER 4
"LOST IT"

February 19, 2015

"Lost it"

Today I lost it over a birdfeeder. (Meaning the sadness was overwhelming and yes, the tears came.) As I was working at the kitchen sink, I saw my empty birdfeeders hanging on their hooks, and slowly but surely …I lost it. Seeing the birdfeeders brought up a past memory of Ben. Ben bought me a birdfeeder for Father's Day several years ago. No, neither of the two feeders I am using now is the one that Ben gave me. That birdfeeder was retired a year ago or so.

The gift was actually from all three of our children, but Ben picked it out and purchased it with the suggestion from his mom that I could use a new birdfeeder. There was nothing special about this birdfeeder. It was made out of plastic like most of the other ones. The only difference was, this one was bigger than most. It could hold more birdseed.

What made the birdfeeder special was Ben. He was so proud that he had picked out and purchased this birdfeeder for me for Father's Day. He knew I enjoyed feeding and watching the birds in our backyard and he thought with a bigger birdfeeder I wouldn't have to fill it as often. There was nothing special about the birdfeeder. It was special because Ben wanted to give me something that he thought I would enjoy. Ben wanted to please me. That was Ben. Seeing the bird feeders in my backyard today brought that memory with all of the emotions and feelings experienced at the time of the gift flooding back. I lost it.

What I am coming to realize more and more is that it is not just the memories of the person and time spent with the person that are so difficult. It is the emotions and feelings experienced during those past experiences that can become overwhelming. It doesn't matter whether those emotions or feelings were positive or negative at the time. It is the memory of the emotions and the feelings that can bring some of the greatest pain and sadness.

It is surprising what simple little things can bring the memories, feelings, and emotions flooding back. Today I lost it over a birdfeeder.

CHAPTER 5
WHEN WE DO NOT KNOW WHAT TO SAY

February 23, 2015

When we do not know what to say

It has now been two months since our son Ben's death. I will not pretend that I have any more answers or any better understanding of mental illness or suicide than I did two months ago. The pain is still deep. I still feel broken. And I don't think there is an hour of the day that goes by that I don't think of and miss Ben.

With that being said I thought I might share some personal reflections on being on the receiving end of consoling. Upon hearing of Ben's death I had someone who had lost a child about Ben's age tell me to be prepared because there would be some well-meaning people who will say some "not so helpful things." This is a common mistake because most of the time we do not know what to say or how to act around someone who has experienced a tragic loss. We would also like to hurry the grieving process for those who are mourning so that life can get back to normal. For those who have lost a loved one, the old "normal" will never be again. Somehow we have to learn to live into our new normal. I write this, not to be critical, but hopefully to be helpful. So here is some of my advice ...at least from my experience. Take it for what it is worth.

First of all, do not try to fix me. I am broken because I have lost someone I loved. I need to be broken. My family will never be complete again for the rest of my life. In that way I will remain broken. I hurt because I love. The deeper the love ...the deeper the pain. In many ways I am almost afraid to lose the pain because I am afraid I will forget the love. My brokenness reminds me of my incompleteness. I am "okay" with that. I hope you are too or at least will respect that.

Secondly, do not tell me that you know my pain or that you know what I am going through. This is a common thing for those who have already lost loved ones. I understand where the comment is coming from as we attempt to make connections with others. It is a way of attempting to stand in solidarity with the one who is in mourning. But pain from the loss of a loved one is directly related to the relationship that one has with the one who has died. So even if you have lost a loved one to suicide, you still do not know my pain any more than I know your pain. My pain is directly related to my relationship with my son. You cannot possibly know or understand my relationship with Ben.

Thirdly, do not tell me that my son is in a better place. I didn't think it was so bad that he was here with us. I would rather have my son with me. Would I take him back from this "better place" if I could? …in a heartbeat. God could have him after I had the rest of my life to enjoy with him.

Fourthly, do not tell me that God must have needed Ben or needed another angel. Look around at creation. Do we really think that a God who created all of this really needs us in heaven? The reality is that with Ben's compassion and concern for people, especially those who are usually left out in society, God could have really used Ben here on earth. Some church or churches just missed out on a really good future pastor. I know I am more than a little biased, but the world is a little worse off without Ben in it. The reality is that the world is a little worse off for every young life that is lost before the full of their potential is achieved.

And lastly, do not be offended when you ask me how I am doing and I respond with, "Functioning." I could tell you that I am doing fine …or good …or okay. The reality is, that that would be a lie. In some ways I am doing fine, good, and okay. In other ways I may never be completely fine, good, or okay. Functioning seems to be the best word that I can use for how I am doing …at least for now. And that is okay with me.

So what do you do to help console those who have lost a loved one? The best thing that I received was just to know that someone cared. Let them know that you are thinking about them and that they are in your prayers. The greatest words I heard spoken were from the people who would say, "I don't know what to say." Their honesty and their compassion meant more to me than anyone who tries to make right or sense of something—that, a person can never do.

Thank you again for letting me share.

Okay, so after the last writing I realized that I have another comment that I heard several times that I did not find helpful. Even though we do not understand why people die unexpectedly, please do not say, "We just do not understand the ways of God." Or "God called your loved one home." It is true that we do not understand the ways of God. But Ben's death had nothing to do with God, other than we are all created human. We are imperfect in our humanity and come with all kinds of physical and mental imperfections. It was not God's will that Ben die in the tragic way in which he did. God did not call Ben home. In faith, I believe that God did welcome him home.

Blessings & peace,
Pastor Keith

August 16, 2018

In the process of putting this book together I realized that I have given some thoughts on what not to do when attempting to console mourners and I really did not give any thoughts on what to do. What to do is really quite simple ...be there. Be present with them in their pain. It is not about you or your past experiences of pain. It is about them and their pain. Know that they are hurting and that you cannot take that pain away no matter what you say or do. The people that I appreciated the most were the people who simply said, "I do not know what to say." It was heart-felt and honest.

Be present and give them space. That might sound like a contradiction but it really is not. Just let them know that you care. You will be there if they need you. Allow them the space to feel free to grieve as they need. It is as simple as that. The simple things can mean a lot. The simple things can also be difficult to do when it comes to matters of consoling someone who is grieving. Your efforts are what will always be remembered and appreciated.

Blessings & peace,
Pastor Keith

CHAPTER 6
"DARK PLACES"

February 23, 2015

"Dark places"

Reflections on mental illness/suicide from a father/pastor

I have been thinking a lot about dark places lately. No, I am not experiencing them. It is the phrase that our son Ben used to describe what he was experiencing when he was in high school. That was the only time that Ben gave any hint to us that he was experiencing mental illness as he never spoke of dark places to Deb and me again. Why Ben kept it hidden from us, I do not know. Maybe he wanted to protect us. Maybe he was afraid of what we and others would think of him. Maybe it was something else. We will never know because the one who could share that is gone. It was Ben's death by suicide in December that made me think of that phrase again. It has in many ways haunted me ever since as I have come to realize that those dark places were a part of Ben's mental illness that he had kept hidden from the rest of us so well.

I confess that I know very little about mental illness, but it seems to me that "dark places" is the best way to describe at least Ben's type of mental illness. For those of us who have never experienced it, it is hard for us to understand or imagine. It must be a place so deep and so dark and so frightening and so hopeless that when one is taken there, there must not seem to be any way out. Again, I cannot imagine what it must feel like for those who experience such a place.

The curse of having a theological education is that one attempts to put things in theological perspective. With suicide, I cannot. But the image of those "dark places" does take me back to the beginning of our Biblical scriptures.

"In the beginning when God created the heavens and the earth, the earth was a formless void and a darkness covered the face of the deep, while a wind from God swept over the face of the waters." Genesis 1:1-2.

It is an image of deep darkness, filled with chaos and uncertainty. It is a frightening place. It sounds like a place that no one would ever choose or want to go. It sounds a lot like what I would envision Ben's image of the "dark places." I wonder now if the writer of the first chapter of Genesis had experienced those dark places. I wonder if he had experienced mental illness.

Of course the writer of Genesis 1 goes on to report that God brought light and order out of the darkness and the chaos in the following verses. But what is even more interesting and reassuring to me in times such as these is that God was present *even in the darkness and the chaos.* "The spirit of God swept over the face of the waters." Deep sea waters were a symbol of chaos and uncertainty in biblical times because no one knew what lay below. I believe and I trust that God was present with Ben when he was experiencing those "dark places" just as God was present in the dark chaos in the beginning. I believe and I trust that God was present with Ben even in his suicide. I believe and I trust that there is not a place that we can go, physically or mentally, that God is not present with us. I find some comfort in that.

For those of us who are left behind, struggling to make sense of the death of a loved one from suicide and attempting to put our lives back in order, I go back to the chaotic verses of Psalm 46.

"God is our refuge and strength, a very present help in trouble. Therefore we will not fear, though the earth should change, though the mountains shake in the heart of the sea; though its waters roar and foam though, the mountains tremble with its tumult." Psalm 46:1-3.

The Psalmist concludes the chapter with: "Be still, and know that I am God! I am exalted among the nations, I am exalted in the earth. The Lord of hosts is with us; the God of Jacob is our refuge." Psalm 46:9-10.

Our world has been shaken to its foundation …and maybe even our faith. One thing is for sure. Our lives are forever changed. I, for one, am still seeking out those quiet places and reassurances.

Thanks again for allowing me to share, Pastor Keith.

CHAPTER 7
"THE THIEF

March 8, 2015

Three months

It has been three months now since our son Ben's death by suicide. Life goes on because that is just the way that life is. As much as we might like it to, life does not hit a pause button while we attempt to deal with our pain and emptiness. We go on with life, not because we want to. That too is just the way it is. We have to carry on… the demands of life dictate it.

Actually, I really do not think that with the death of a loved one a person actually moves on. I have often heard someone comment about someone who has lost a loved one, "Well, at some point they just need to move on." I do not think that a person ever moves on. Moving on makes it sound like they have moved past the pain and the emptiness that the death of a loved one has left behind. That pain and the emptiness might ease some, but a person never moves completely past it.

The reality is I do not want to ever "move on." I do not want to "move on" past the memories of the loved one lost. I do not want to "move on" past the love that was shared. I do not want to "move on" past missing that person. I do not want to "move on."

What life does dictate though is that a person must move forward. We have to move forward into our lives without our loved one. We have to move forward into our new normal. The rest of the world moves on. We have to learn, somehow, to move forward. `

The thief

Silently it comes, the thief in the night
Violently it steals, keeping out of sight
Leaving behind destruction and pain
Lives that will never be the same again

It steals the happiness that once was there
In its wake leaves sadness beyond compare
It takes with it the joy and leaves the strife
Death is the thief that takes more than life

Keith C Kraft October 29, 2017

CHAPTER 8
FIRST EASTER RAMBLINGS

April 5, 2015

First Easter ramblings

Today I wore my new suit for the first time to church for Easter services. There would usually be nothing significant about that other than I usually do not pay attention to those kinds of details. I buy new clothing and I wear it. It usually isn't anything special. The difference this time is that the last two suits I bought and the first time I wore them was at each of our two children's weddings. I was hoping and planning on doing the same for Ben's wedding and carrying on that tradition. Reality had other ideas.

As those of you who have lost loved ones know, holidays are particularly difficult. Easter is a time that we would have seen Ben at some point during this weekend. If we wouldn't have seen him here at home, we would have seen him when we went to our daughter and son-in-law's on Sunday evening.

But as a pastor, at least for me, Easter brings with it an extra challenge. How do you preach resurrection joy when you are not feeling it? I apologize to my congregation and to those who came to visit our worship if they came expecting to hear a joyous message. And yet, maybe it is those who have lost loved ones recently who can best understand what the disciples, including the women who went to the tomb that first Easter morning, were feeling and experiencing. I know for me, I can best relate to the women in Mark's version of that first Easter morning who ran away from the empty tomb in fear and wonder. The joy and the rejoicing will come. It will just have to wait another year. I am sure that God will understand.

To all who read this: I hope you have a blessed Easter. I truly hope that you do experience the risen Christ some time during this Easter season.

The first Easter

(After the death of a loved one)

How do you experience resurrection joy
When all you feel is the pain of loss?
How do you live into future hope
When today's hopes have all been tossed?

How do you celebrate newness of life
When your life is filled with emptiness?
These are answers I do not have
It is to this, that I confess.

And yet the realities of life dictate
Somehow we must move forward.
So the best advice that I can give is:
Look and learn from the risen Lord.

From Jesus I've learned each and every day
That on this earth I trod
While it might seem over simplified
I place my faith …in God.

Keith C Kraft April 5, 2015

CHAPTER 9
A FACE OF MENTAL ILLNESS

April 9, 2015

The first graveside visit

Today I went to Wessington Springs to take care of some personal business. There is nothing really significant about that in and of itself. What some of you might not realize is that Wessington Springs is Deb's and my hometown. The Wessington Springs cemetery is also where we had our son Ben buried. I haven't been back to Wessington Springs other than a quick pass through to see Dad around Christmas. It never really hit me how hard this trip would be until I was about half way to Wessington Springs. Being tired and alone didn't help the emotions any.

I had a hard time just driving by the road that led to the cemetery when we passed through Wessington Springs at Christmas time. This time I felt that I needed to go see Ben's gravesite. I really didn't want to, but for some reason, I needed to. Once I got there it was a little difficult to leave. Maybe if the wind wouldn't have been blowing so hard and the fact that I needed to get on the long road home, I might have lingered longer. I might have asked some questions that I know I wouldn't have received any answers to. I might have tried to capture the feeling of being close to Ben …at least the last place we had laid Ben's body to rest. I might have contemplated the meaning of life, which again, I know I wouldn't have come up with any good answers.

As I stood there and looked at the mound of dirt that now covers Ben's grave I was reminded of how precious life really is …and how fragile. Wishing you all blessings and peace this Easter season, Pastor Keith

April 12, 2015

Another face of Mental Illness: depression and anxiety

There are many faces of mental illness: depression and anxiety. Many you would not recognize as such. They look like regular people going about their normal activities of life. And they are just that--only they carry with them a dark secret deep within them. It is a secret that they keep hidden and masked. It is a secret that only a few others who are close to them might see or experience. But for most of us it is hidden away ...locked inside of our loved ones ...buried deep within until it can no longer be contained.

This picture of Ben was taken in Colorado in the summer of 2010 when we were on vacation. Whether Ben was suffering from one of his episodes of depression or anxiety at this time, I do not know and Ben is not around to tell us. My guess is that the mental illness was always there. It is just that the effects of it are stronger at certain times. I do not know. But what I do know is that the face that you see in the picture is the face that we saw most of the time. Oh sure, we saw the occasional face of frustration, reflection, and even some anger at times. But nothing more than anyone else. The face you see in this picture is the face that we usually saw. Ben never let us in to see the pain and despair of depression and anxiety.

The point is: the face of depression that you see on TV advertisements for depression medicine is not the only face that is out there. Many of those who are suffering from mental illness, depression, and anxiety do not show the usual signs that most of us think of as signs of mental illness. Many mental illness victims mask their symptoms and carry on with life quite normally. It is not until the illness gets to be more than they can bear that the truth of the illness shows its ugly head in ways that most of us do not and will not ever understand.

My hope is that at some point there will be a time when those who are suffering from mental illness will not feel like they have to keep it masked from the rest of us, especially the ones who love them. It begins with caring, talking honestly and openly, and listening without judgment or criticism.

Ben, you are so missed. To the rest of you, blessing and peace, Pastor Keith

CHAPTER 10
DEFINING THE LINE

April 21, 2015

Defining the line

One of the things that I have been struggling with the past several months since Ben's death is trying to figure out how one defines the line where depression and anxiety can possibly lead to suicide. I would venture to guess that all of us feel depressed from time to time. All of us feel anxious periodically. Some might even feel depressed and anxious to the point where it affects our home and work life but still would not necessarily consider taking the step of suicide. I would guess that all of us could plot our depression and anxiety on a line from normal, to this is a problem, to this is a serious problem.

It seems to me that the key would be to recognize the line where a person is no longer controlling the depression and anxiety, but rather when the depression and anxiety are controlling the person. The next step is where the depression and anxiety are controlling to the point where a person would harm oneself. The real challenge is to recognize and acknowledge where and when that line of absolutely no control is before it is too late. Once a person has crossed that line there is no rationalizing and most of the time, no return. The difficult thing is that the only person who can tell where that line is, is the person who is experiencing the depression and anxiety. I even wonder if they really know where that line is.

I am no mental health expert by any stretch of the imagination. I am simply a distraught father trying to make sense of something that I will probably never make sense of. The only advice I can give is this: if you are questioning if you might cross over the line, please seek professional help …for your sake and the sake of your loved ones.

Brokenness and Pain

We are not unique
We all belong, you and me
It's just the way it is, you see
It's a part of human reality
We belong to the broken family
Sad and empty from loved ones gone
Left to attempt to struggle on

So those of us who experience pain
And emptiness again and again
Must know our pain is not unique
Nor are we the only ones who seek
Answers, compassion and reassurance
And from the depth of pain, deliverance

For others I do truly empathize
But you must also realize
My pain *is* my pain
While like others, many ways the same
It is still my pain, so you see
In that way, it is for me,
...like your pain
...unique

Keith C Kraft February 26, 2015

CHAPTER 11
LIFE, DEATH, AND FEEDING BIRDS

April 22, 2015

MISYA explained

April 2015 we organized our first MISYA walk, (Mental Illness, Suicide Yearly Awareness walk.) Our walk is mainly to raise awareness and education around the issues of mental illness and suicide. If people do choose to donate money it is given to the American Foundation for Suicide Prevention in Ben's name. The following further explains the meaning of the acronym.

The acronym MISYA speaks more than what one might first think. Of course it speaks for those of us who have lost loved ones to mental illness through suicide. But it also speaks for those who have loved ones currently dealing with mental illness. During bouts of mental illness a person just isn't the person they really are. The mental illness robs them of their real personality and vigor for life. I have a former seminary professor who told me his son took off for a year and a half and they had no idea where he was. Through suicide, mental illness has a way of robbing the loved ones of suicide victims of their real personalities and vigor for life as well. Mental illness has a way of taking away our loved ones in many different ways.

It is to those who have lost their struggle with mental illness through suicide, those who are still struggling with mental illness, and to the families and loved ones of both that we say, "We miss you." It is for you that we walk.

April 26, 2015

Life, death, & feeding birds

Yesterday we had our first annual Mental Illness, Suicide Yearly Awareness walk. We had a nice turnout of around 65 people. I hope people will continue to come and support the walk in the coming years. We know all too well that mental illness and suicide is not just a one-time event. Mental illness and suicide, though not often talked about, are prevalent in our society. The next event that Deb and I have been asked to participate in is a suicide prevention training this Sunday, May 3rd in Rapid City for a National Guard Unit that is preparing to deploy this coming August.

As I am thinking about this and what we have done these past few months there is just something in my brain that wants to scream, "This is crazy! This is absolutely insane! I shouldn't be organizing walks for mental illness and suicide awareness. I shouldn't be receiving phone calls from South Dakota National Guard lieutenants from another part of the state. We shouldn't be talking to some 500 high school students about suicide and mental illness. This is not who I am. This is not who we are. This is not who I want to be. We should be helping to organize our son's college graduation reception. We should be talking to our son about which seminary to attend or help work through what he wants to do with his future. Not this …this is absolutely nuts."

I have started feeding the birds again this spring. It is something that I have kind of neglected the past couple of years. With so many of my thoughts being on the death of our son, I decided that our backyard needed some life in it. I was quickly reminded of what a mess feeding birds makes in your yard. There are sunflower seeds all over the ground and birds scratching around trying to get the feed that has fallen out of the feeders. It really is a mess. I was also quickly reminded that you will also get birds that you do not necessarily care for. Once you put bird feed out, you cannot choose which birds can and which birds cannot come to your feeder.

Such is life. We cannot always choose what will land on our doorstep. There is much in this world that is beyond our control. We have to take the bad along with the good. I am also reminded of something one of my seminary professors used to say and Ben's death adds the exclamation points. "Life is messy!!" The best that we can do at times is to somehow struggle to learn how to live in and through the messiness of life.

Blessings and peace,
Pastor Keith.

CHAPTER 12
DEAR BEN

April 29, 2015

Dear Ben,

I wrote a couple of letters to you while you were in Afghanistan as a way of helping process some things that were going through my mind. Here I am again doing the same. Besides, I have heard it said that it is good therapy for those who are grieving to write letters to their loved ones who have died. Whether that is true or not, I do not know.

I do know that I find myself many times wishing I could talk to you and wishing that you could help me better understand this thing that we call suicide. There are times that I wish you could share with me those things that were going through your mind and what you were experiencing all of these years. And then there are other times that I think that it is probably better that I do not know. If the things that were going through your mind that final night and many other times before were so dark …so hideous …so hopeless …so frightening that it drove you to take your own life, than maybe it is better for me as your parent not to know the horrifying details.

And yet there is something in my mind that keeps screaming (I have had a lot of things screaming in my mind lately) that we are missing the point of understanding suicide. The topic of suicide on the reservation has come up on the news a couple of times these past few weeks. It is an issue of major concern especially among the Native youth. The response seems to be to plan fun recreational activities for the youth. It is the hope to show them that life can be fun …to give them some hope. These are positive and helpful things and I used to think that that was the answer too. If we could eliminate poverty and hopelessness then we could eliminate at least most of the suicide issues.

Sadly, you have shown me that there is more to suicide than that. You were not faced with the hopelessness, at least not in the economic sense like so many on the reservation face. There was a world of possibilities open to you. You enjoyed life and took advantage of many of the opportunities that were open to you. You did not face many of the issues that so many of our brothers and sisters on the reservations face. The future was bright and full of possibilities for you. Yet the result of suicide is the same as so many of our young brothers and sisters on the reservation who might not have seen a bright future full of possibilities. And so I am left to reason that there is more to suicide than just broken families, poverty, and hopelessness.

But since I do not have you to help me understand what you were going through, I can only ponder and guess. It is my thinking at this point of my struggling to understand that at least the majority of suicide is the result of mental illness amplified and brought to culmination by stressors such as, but not limited to things like broken families, poverty, and hopelessness. But there are many other stressors in our lives as well. Many of these are common events like broken relationship, stress on the job, money concerns, occupational changes, career choices, and the list could go on. Most people experience these things as a reality of life. There are other stressors that are not common to most people such as being called to war, experiencing tragic events, being under investigation, and others as well.

I guess my point is that I do not believe that it is just the stressors alone that cause most suicides. It is the combination of the mental illness such as depression, anxiety, schizophrenia, bipolar or other mental illness, spurred on by some stressor or other that the person is experiencing at that particular point in his or her life.

My concern is that we are not recognizing the complexity of the suicide problem. We are only trying to deal with the cosmetics of the issue. We think if people are happy with life, then they won't commit suicide. We can say things like, "Suicide is a permanent solution to a temporary problem" and think that once people recognize that that they won't commit suicide. My mind screams "No!" because you knew all of that …at least when you weren't in those dark places. It is the mental illness that causes one not to think rationally.

Anyway, I wish you were here to tell me if I was even close in my thinking or if I was clearly off base. It would be nice to know, partly to help me to better understand your death, and partly so that I can possibly help bring understanding to others. Maybe through better understanding we can begin to prevent some of these tragic and unnecessary deaths.

I know that you cannot give me an answer so I guess this one I will have to muddle through on my own. I do miss our honest talks and conversations. Know that your family misses you very much. Your mom and I are doing the best we can. We miss you dearly. We trust that you are at peace and that God has brought light into those dark places.

Peace as only God can give,
Keith aka Dad

CHAPTER 13
"OPEN MY EYES"

June 20, 2015

"Open my eyes"

"Open my eyes, that I may see Glimpses of truth thou hast for me;
Place in my hands the wonderful key that shall unclasp and set me free."[1]

Sadly, why is it that sometimes it seems that we have to be hit up the side of the head with a blunt object before we open our eyes? I have heard of suicides all of my life, although not nearly as often as I have in the last fifteen years. I, like most everyone else, rationalized them in some way or other. It's a reservation issue. It's a silly young person issue. It's a poor coping skills issue. I was also fully aware of mental illness: schizophrenia, bi-polar, severe depression, etc. …you know the ones when they are really obvious. I felt sorry for those who had to deal with those things in their families and thankful it wasn't in mine. I never really gave it much thought to connect the two …suicide with mental illness. And then reality opened my eyes with a personal tragedy in the family.

It grieves me to think that it took the unexpected death of my son to open my eyes to begin to see the truth about the connection between mental illness and suicide. But if it doesn't affect me personally, I just don't concern myself with it too much. I have other things to worry about. I would venture to guess that I am not unique in this. I would guess that that is the way for many of us. It doesn't affect us so we don't bother getting too concerned with the issue.

"Open my eyes," is really my purpose for sharing this blog. I know that most of what I have shared is my pain and my journey through that pain, (which is and will continue to be an ongoing journey.) But my real purpose is to help open the eyes and ears of those who read these words to the reality of mental illness and suicide, and the pain and isolation that it can bring to the individuals and families who suffer from their effects. It does not matter to me that you become an advocate for mental illness and suicide issues. My only hope for you who read these words is that you become aware of their reality. They are more prevalent than most of us are aware. And they can happen in any family. My deepest prayer for you is that you never have to experience a personal tragedy in your family to open your eyes.

The words to the hymn that I opened with were written in the 1800s by Clara H. Scott. It is a prayerful hymn. It is my prayer for you and for me, not only to open our eyes, ears, mouths, and hearts to those dealing with mental illness, but to all matters of pain and misunderstandings. May we become more aware and more sensitive to the issues that others are dealing with in their lives.

Open my eyes, that I may see Glimpses of truth thou hast for me;
Place in my hands the wonderful key that shall unclasp and set me free.

Refrain: Silently now I wait for thee, Ready my God thy will to see;
Open my eyes illumine me, Spirit divine!

Open my ears, that I may hear Voices of truth thou sendest clear;
And while the wave-notes fall on my ear, Everything false will disappear.
Refrain:
Open my mouth, and let me bear Gladly the warm truth everywhere
Open my heart and let me prepare Love with thy children thus to share.[1]

Oh, and Happy Father's Day.
My Father's Day wish is that Ben will not be forgotten.

Blessings and peace,
Pastor Keith

CHAPTER 14
REFLECTIONS OF A SELF-PORTRAIT

August 6, 2015

Reflections of a Self-portrait

National Geographic started a project along with a book to encourage amateur photographers to improve their skills in the art of photography. Every so often they would put out a new challenge with a specific theme. One of those themes was to encourage amateur photographers to take a self-portrait, i.e. a picture of themselves or something that reflected who they were.

As I was thinking about what picture would best give people a look at how I see myself right now, I realized something I already knew. The reality is that life circumstances and events really shape who we are at a given time. But I also realize that this photograph is not the complete picture nor is this photograph the last picture of a self-portrait of me. I know that this photograph will fade some with time. Other events in my life will happen that will begin to come into play in my life that will cause this picture not to have quite as much impact on who I am. Other events will help to lessen the impact of this one event.

One thing that will not change is that the event of the death of our son Ben will always be there. It will continue to have an impact on the rest of my life. I am forever changed. Ben's death and the event of Ben's suicide will always be a part of who I am. That will never change. Like a photograph taken at a specific time at a specific event, the event of Ben's death and the impact that it has on the rest of my life can never be changed. It might fade some. It might dim, but you can never change the content of the photograph.

CHAPTER 15
"THE ZINNIA"

August 26, 2015

Out of the depths I cry to you, O Lord, [2] Lord, hear my voice!
Let your ears be attentive to the voice of my supplications!

Psalm 130:1-2

The Zinnia

There are days I just want to sit in the quiet sanctuary of my God (wherever that might be) and ask God, "Why?" This is not an angry question on my part because I know that Ben's death was not a part of God's plan. But yet my heart still cries out in pain, "Why? Why? …why?" It is the cry and the questions of a broken heart still in much pain. I realize that it must have been great pain that drove Ben to the act of suicide …and my pain grows deeper. "Why?" Although my faith says otherwise, the question seems to fall on deaf or uncaring ears.

It is not long that my questions turn to looking for reassurance. I desperately desire to know that my son is "okay." When he was here I could call or text him to ask him if he was "okay." There were times when I was around him I could sense that he was troubled by something. I could ask him. I could try to give counsel. I could try to give reassurance. I could, if nothing else, let him know that I loved him and I really did care about him and his well-being. Now that we are separated by this vast thing that we call death I can no longer do that. I feel the need to know that he is all right. I want to know. …I am only greeted with heavy silence. I want to hear a word of reassurance. I hear only silence.

This past summer I planted zinnias along our driveway as I always have …three rows of them. What was unusual this year is that practically one whole row of them never even germinated. Only a couple plants came up in one complete row. Disgusted because of the time that it would take and unsure if they would take root, I thinned some of the plants from the other two rows and transplanted them to the empty row. It worked. My zinnia flower bed looks full with no hint of the original setback. I was pleased with my success.

I was mowing my lawn in late July when I noticed a purple flower had bloomed in probably the ugliest part of my yard …right where the concrete of the driveway, the roughly patched asphalt of the city street, the broken concrete of the curb, and the weeds from the yard because nothing else will grow there, come together. It was a zinnia. It is some 20 feet and across the concrete driveway from my other zinnias. It is where nothing but weeds usually grow. It is where I always mow. I had a difficult time getting some of my zinnias to grow where I wanted them to grow and yet here in this odd place and against the odds, this flower has not only grown, but has also bloomed. How it got there and why it grew there, I will never know.

I am not sure what it all means or if God is trying to teach me a lesson in this or not, but I cannot seem to bring myself to mow over it. Maybe it is a symbol of hope that God can bring new life to dark, ugly, unexpected places. At least that is the hope that I am holding onto. At any rate, I figure if God planted the zinnia there then God must have wanted it there. I didn't plant it there. I would have picked a better spot. So there it sits …all by itself right next to the street, probably noticed by very few. If nothing else this one zinnia has shown me one thing--as much as I would like to be and as much as I try to be, I am not in control. I just have to wait and see what God will bring out of the chaos and uncertainty that we call life.

I would still like the answer to my questions of "why" …why Ben's death and mental illness. I would still like the reassurance that Ben is "okay." But for now a zinnia sits at the corner of my yard where the concrete driveway and the asphalt street meet trying to bring beauty under some difficult circumstances.

Blessings & peace,
Pastor Keith

September 28, 2015

The Zinnia – the continuing story

So this is a continuation of the story of the oddly placed zinnia. What many of you do not realize is that there was a week between the time that I wrote about the zinnia and the time that I put the story on the website and in the newsletter. In between writing and posting, Mobridge experienced a 50 mph plus wind over the weekend while Deb and I were gone. Upon returning I found my oddly placed zinnia pulled out of the ground. It was barely hanging on by the tips of its roots. The only flower that had bloomed on the plant had been ripped off. The plant looked terrible and I, surprisingly, found myself feeling sad over the loss of the flower. This simple, oddly-placed flower had brought little pieces of joy into my life and now it was gone. I know it seems trivial, but I missed the flower.

I was also concerned that I had written an article about this zinnia flower and now there was no flower. What would people say if they read the newsletter article, drove by my driveway, and now the flower is gone? With very little hope I took what was left of the plant, propped it up as best as I could, and took my thumb, pushing the roots of the plant back into the quarter-inch shallow soil. Underneath the soil was asphalt. I wasn't holding my breath.

Much to my surprise and joy, the day that we mailed the newsletter out with my poorly-timed article on the zinnia, another bud opened up. I kid you not, there is once again a zinnia flower sitting at the end of my driveway bringing a little beauty to an otherwise ugly looking part of my yard. The plant looks a little odd as it is bent and crooked. But the flower is there at the end of my driveway greeting me every time I come home or mow my lawn.

I imagine you could get several metaphors out of this little story like the resiliency that God has created within nature to recover after being whipped around by life's storms. As part of God's creation, God has given us that same resiliency to weather our storms of life. Or there could be the metaphor that sometimes what we need during difficult times is a little help from a loving and caring hand. We are not alone in this world and sometimes we need the help of friends to keep us grounded. Or another metaphor could be that we need to keep our faith rooted in God to withstand many of the things that life throws our way. There will be times when we feel like our faith is barely hanging on by the fingertips. But even that can keep us rooted in God.

All of these metaphors would be appropriate and there might even be more. As for me, the zinnia is a reminder of the amazing mysteries and wonders of God and God's creation. There is much that I do not know and do not understand. And I am okay with that. At least for now I am learning to be "okay" with that. It is called living in faith into an unknown future and living with a past that we cannot change.

I know that with fall here and winter right around the corner, the days for that flower are numbered. It won't be long and it too will wither and die. When that happens I am sure that I will be a little sad again. It is called life. But for now I once again have a purple zinnia flower sitting at the end of my driveway bringing me little pieces of joy, a smile to my face, and a wonder in my heart whenever I see it. That too is life.

Sometimes we have to look for the little pieces of joy and happiness whenever and wherever we can find them …even in the seemingly simple, oddly placed, and odd looking things of life.

Peace & blessings,
Pastor Keith

CHAPTER 16
MORE RAMBLINGS AFTER 10 MONTHS

October, 28, 2015

More ramblings after ten months

The first anniversary of Ben's death is quickly approaching. I am no closer to understanding suicide or mental illness than I was ten months ago. I can only still surmise that the two are related …at least in Ben's case. I am convinced that there would not have been a suicide without the mental illness. Maybe there are cases where suicides have occurred without the mental illness, but it would take some persuading to convince me. What I do know is that those of us who have never experienced the "dark places" that Ben spoke about in high school and obviously followed him after high school will never ever fully understand what that experience is like. We can only imagine, and even that makes me shiver.

Ben's death has given me a greater awareness of what the families who have lost loved ones are going through. As a pastor, I have the privilege of being invited into the pain and the grief of family members as they journey through the death of a loved one. I have always thought that I was at least fairly compassionate and empathetic. I have always thought that I was a fairly understanding person. After all, I have experienced the loss of a mother and a mother-in-law. After Ben's death I realized that I was absolutely clueless to the depth of pain that family members could be experiencing.

Thankfully for me, I still do not know what it is like to lose a beloved spouse. For those who have, you have my utmost respect and sympathy. For those of you to whom I have ministered in the past, I apologize. I did not and could not know the depth of your pain. I realize that each person's experience of pain and sorrow is unique depending on the person and the relationship to the one who has died. But I do have a better understanding now of pain that can cut to the core of one's being. In the words of the television character, *Monk*, "It is a blessing and a curse." …with emphasis on "curse."

One thing that has surprised me about traveling through this grieving process is that it seems that as I get closer to the anniversary of Ben's death it is once again getting more difficult to cope with things. The emotions are getting stronger and yet sometimes it seems like there are times when there is no emotion at all. It seems that there are no tears left to cry …only an empty hollow feeling. …nothing …emotionless …and then guilt for feeling emotionless. And at other times the tears are hard to hold back.

What is common is the anxiety and dread of facing the coming days. I can only rationalize that it is because we are coming to the "last of the firsts." In the next two months we are facing: my first deer hunt without Ben in several years other than when he was deployed in Afghanistan; our first Thanksgiving without Ben which was the last time we were all together as a family; Ben's birthday; the anniversary of Ben's death; our first Christmas without Ben. (I'll be honest. I don't remember much of last Christmas other than pain and sorrow.)

I think another reason for the anxiety is that as a person gets farther away from the death of a loved one it is easy to feel a little more alone and isolated in your grief. Almost everyone else has moved on …which is to be expected. They are not as close to your loved one as you are. The other thing is that everyone else wants you to move on as well. This too is normal. It is not because they are unsympathetic. It is because they want things to be back to "normal" and things will not be back to "normal" until you are "normal." The reality is that you will never be back to the way you once were before the death. One has to learn to live into a new normal.

For those of you who take the time to read these ramblings I hope you know that I do not write them to illicit sympathy. My purpose is really fourfold. First and foremost, I write as a way to help me process what I am thinking, feeling, and experiencing. Second, I write these words so that I might not forget. I hope it will help me continue to grow in compassion and understanding as a pastor.

Thirdly, I write for those of you who might be or probably some day will be going through the same experience of the loss of a loved one. I know that my experience might be unique to me, but pain is universal when it comes to losing a loved one. I hope that maybe these thoughts will help you process what you have, are, or will be going through. In the end, my prayer is that you will experience some comfort and peace through these writings. Fourthly, I hope these words serve as a reminder that mental illness and suicide are real in our society. Mental illness is not a sign of weakness and suicide is not an easy way out …not for the victim …not for the families left behind.

Blessings & peace,
Pastor Keith.

CHAPTER 17
THE ROAD ALONE

November 2, 2015

Totenfest 2015

Today I took off my Alb and my stole during worship. We celebrated *Totenfest* as part of worship service today. *Totenfest* is when we read the names and light a candle for members of our church who have passed away this past year. We also read the names and light a candle for each of the baptisms and births from our church this past year. The deacons of our church take the leadership and I usually just sit. What was unique about this year is that it was the year our son Ben's name would be spoken. We also had communion as part of the worship service.

I performed the usual parts of our worship service in my usual attire, wearing my stole with my Alb. *Totenfest* was the last part of worship service following communion other than the final hymn. After communion I took off my Alb, my stole, and my mic, and I went to sit with my wife Deb and with the rest of the congregation. I took off the role of pastor. I am not sure that the rest of the congregation got the symbolism but it was important to me to sit with Deb without my Alb and stole. Today I was a supportive spouse and a grieving parent.

Blessings & peace,
Pastor Keith

The road alone

Share my grief with me
Know my pain
Feel my sadness
That comes again and again

Experience the loss
And the empty hole
That dwells within
The depths of my soul

Oh, but sadly
It is not to be
For the grief is mine
It is my reality

Reality says
That you cannot share
That which I alone
Can only bear

You can share words
Of comfort and hope
For which I am grateful
For they help me cope

But when it comes to grief
As many have known
It is a road
I must walk alone

Keith C Kraft August 3, 2017

CHAPTER 18
ONE FINAL LESSON FROM THE ZINNIA

November 16, 2015

One final lesson from my oddly placed zinnia

Well, my zinnia finally died. Last weekend's freezing temperatures were too much for it and it finally died. I knew this day would come. I knew that the zinnia would not last all winter. So it is with the ways of nature and plants in South Dakota. They grow in the summer and die with the coming of winter. I know it. I knew it. And still, in some odd way, it makes me a little sad.

Most of you know what I am talking about with my zinnia. For those of you who do not, I have a zinnia which had chosen to grow at the end of my driveway in an odd place where I never planted it. The zinnias that I planted were some twenty feet away and even some of those that I planted didn't want to grow. And yet here in this odd place is this odd zinnia plant that has graced my yard for much of the summer and fall. In an odd way it has been my yard companion. It has been there when I came home, or went to get the mail, or mowed my lawn.

With a little help, this zinnia has withstood fifty-mile-an-hour winds. It has sprung back to life after it had been all but ripped out of the ground and barely hanging on by the tips of its roots. We protected it from weed spray. In the midst of everything with the death of our son last winter, this zinnia, in some odd way that I cannot explain has been a source of comfort, wonder, and beauty, and a symbol of hope and resilience. And now it is dead. Like I said, I knew it was coming, but it is still a little sad. I really should pull the dead plant, but for some odd reason I just can't bring myself to do it. Even though it is dead and brown, it still is a reminder to me of the source of wonder and beauty, and a symbol of hope and resilience that it once was. To remove it would be to remove that reminder and that symbol.

With the changing of times I am reminded of Apostle Paul's letter to the Roman church. In times of uncertainty and change our only real hope is in that which we cannot see …in that which is eternal and will not wither and die. Our hope is in God and God's love and grace.

[18] I consider that the sufferings of this present time are not worth comparing with the glory about to be revealed to us. [19] For the creation waits with eager longing for the revealing of the children of God; [20] for the creation was subjected to futility, not of its own will but by the will of the one who subjected it, in hope [21] that the creation itself will be set free from its bondage to decay and will obtain the freedom of the glory of the children of God. [22] We know that the whole creation has been groaning in labor pains until now; [23] and not only the creation, but we ourselves, who have the first fruits of the Spirit, groan inwardly while we wait for adoption, the redemption of our bodies. [24] For in hope we were saved. Now hope that is seen is not hope. For who hopes for what is seen?"
Romans 8:18-24

There will always be pain, suffering, and uncertainty as long as we are journeying through this thing that we call life. Nothing lasts forever. Sin and death are a part of the human condition. Earthly things crumble and decay and are replaced by other earthly things which crumble and decay. The only one that is eternal is God. The only thing that lasts forever is the love and grace of God. It is in God and in God's presence that we must put our faith and our trust …and our hope. It has to be. It has to be …because there is nothing else.

Blessings & peace,
Pastor Keith

CHAPTER 19
LAST OF THE FIRSTS

December 8, 2015

Last of the firsts

Today was the last of the firsts for our family. Today is the first anniversary of our son Ben's death from suicide. Last year December 8th meant nothing to me. It was just another day. The day that Ben died I couldn't have told you what day it was other than that it was a Monday. Now I will never forget December 8th or how it changed my imagined, ordered world. The pain will ease with time. The memory of the pain of that day might even fade some, but I doubt that it will ever be forgotten.

Deb and I commemorated the day by closing the church, skipping work, and going to Wessington Springs to visit Ben's grave. It also gave us the chance to see my dad and step-mom as well as one of my brothers and his wife. It was good to see them. My brother brought my dad to the gravesite. It was good to have him there. While showing Dad the veteran's plaque on the back of the grave marker, I mentioned that Ben was proud of his service in the National Guard and his service overseas in Afghanistan. Dad nodded in agreement. It was, I believe, my dad's way of saying that he was proud of Ben too. A stroke has taken my dad's ability to talk.

It has been a good, difficult, and emotional day. The day has brought back many memories of that day one year ago. In some ways the emotion and the pain are almost just as raw as they were when we received the news of Ben's death. I can still hear the phone ringing at 5:00 in the morning and Sgt. Heil's voice saying, "Keith, I need to talk to you." I can still feel the dread building within me as I went to the door, knowing that no news is good news when it comes from someone outside of your family during the darkness of night. I can still feel my heart sinking when I opened the door to Sgt. Heil with Officer Mewjeski soberly standing behind him. I can still feel the shock, disbelief, and numbness when they gave Deb and me the news of Ben's death and how he died. I can still vividly remember those first reactions of our children and Mike when I told them the news: disbelief, sobs, and silence. It still breaks my heart when I remember.

A year later it is still hard for me to believe. It is hard to accept the fact that this young man who was so happy most of the time …had so much promise …had so many plans …was so bright in so many ways …had so much compassion for others …enjoyed people and life, and had so much to live for could possibly take his own life. There are times I still expect him to show up at my door, text me or call me on the phone, and yet… reality says otherwise.

Even though I am pretty much convinced that Ben's death was caused by a mental illness of which we were not fully aware, there are times that I still question. I question whether I was a good parent? Did I pressure Ben too much one way or another? Did I not take enough interest in his life? What did I do that Ben was not comfortable enough to share this horrible secret with me? For the most part probably foolish questions which I do not spend a lot of time on, but still they are there.

The reality is, for the most part I feel that I am doing pretty well …as long as I don't stop and think about it too long. What kills me inside the most is when I think about the actual event of Ben's death. There is great pain in thinking about the pain that Ben must have been in that lonely, dark night and the violent nature of that death. I cannot stay in that place too long. I am still broken and always will be. I have come to accept that and that is okay with me. For Ben, I will gladly remain broken even as I know that healing will come.

So how have I changed since Ben's death? I am more emotional. I have always been somewhat emotional, but it is worse now. I choke up and the tears come easier. It is more difficult for me to watch television shows and movies that are emotional, whether they are happy or sad. Even the news with all of the death reports are harder to watch. It is harder to leave my other two kids after we have seen them. What used to be something I always took for granted, now I get emotional inside and tear up a little when we say good-bye. (I try not to let them know.)

In some ways I am less tolerant of some things and some people that I feel like are obsessing or fretting over what I feel are insignificant things. In other ways I am more appreciative of other people. There are so many people that I would like to thank but to name you all and how you are special to me through this past year would go on for too long and I would probably leave somebody out. I think, at least I hope you all know. I hope I have told you and shown you. I wish I could give you all a hug (and I am not the kind of person who normally cares to hug) …another change.

I know I will remain broken. I know that the healing is coming and will continue to come. I hope and pray that society will continue to grow in understanding and awareness to the connection between mental illness and suicide.

Ben, you are so missed. I just wish...

Blessings & peace,
Pastor Keith

December 9, 2015

Yesterday was the last of the firsts for our family. Yesterday was the anniversary of our son Ben's death. If you would like to read more thoughts on yesterday's experience you can go to our church website. This will be the last time that I will be posting on Facebook thoughts and reflections on my personal experience of the grieving process from losing a son to suicide. I will still write as the Spirit moves me to write as part of my continued grieving process. I will still post those writings on our church's website for those who might want to venture that way as a means of keeping in touch or if it helps with their healing process. But I will not be using Facebook to let you know when they happen. It is time for me to continue my grieving in a manner that I am much more comfortable with …quietly and privately. Thank you for your words of comfort and support throughout this past year. As always, continued blessings and peace. Pastor Keith.

CHAPTER 20
THE SECOND CHRISTMAS SEASON

December 21, 2015

Longest Night worship service
December 21, 2015

Meditation

Genesis 1:1-2

In the beginning when God created the heavens and the earth, [2] the earth was a formless void and darkness covered the face of the deep, while a wind from God swept over the face of the waters.

I'm going to pause there. I'm going to pause there because I want you to hear these words again, not just as a creation story as we are so used to hearing them as, but I want you to hear them as a description of life in general. Many Biblical scholars figure that this first creation story was written at a time when ancient Israel was in exile or had just returned from exile. They were experiencing a time of chaos and uncertainty. The future ahead looked dark and scary. Waters, in ancient times, were a symbol of chaos and uncertainty. You never knew what lurked below the surface of the waters. They were dark, dangerous and uncertain. When you were out on big bodies of water, storms could come up unexpectedly and swallow you up. Such is life …chaotic and uncertain where storms can come up unexpectedly. So hear these words again.

"In the beginning when God created the heavens and the earth, [2] the earth was a formless void and darkness covered the face of the deep, while a wind from God swept over the face of the waters."

That might be where many of us, or at least some of us gathered here tonight, are at right now …or at least, feel like that is where we are at right now. We feel like that formless void …this emptiness within us with no real directions. Life has no real shape to it. There is this sense of darkness that covers us. There is this sense of chaos and uncertainty in our lives. For whatever reason, that might be where we are at in life right now. That is okay. That is not a bad place to be. It is good for us to acknowledge where we are. If we are in that chaotic, uncertain, scary dark place, then we need to claim it. And it is even okay to remain there, at least for a little while. It is okay to be there because into this chaotic, uncertain, scary, darkness the writer of the first chapter of Genesis brings us a twofold message of Good News.

The first message of Good News is that God is present. God is present in the mess and the brokenness of our lives. The same wind of God or Spirit of God that was present in the beginning of creation when all was dark and chaotic is the Spirit of God that is present with us in our dark and uncertain times. We must remember that. Even when we do not feel God's presence, God is still present. Even in our darkest, most hopeless times of our lives, God is present with us.

The second message of Good News comes in verses 3 and 4.
3 Then God said, "Let there be light"; and there was light. 4
And God saw that the light was good; and God separated the light from the darkness."

Into this chaotic, uncertain, scary, darkness, God speaks, "Let there be light." And there was light and God separated the light from the darkness. God is working to bring order out of chaos. God is not only present with us in our times of uncertainty and chaos, but God is also working to help bring back order into our lives. It will not come quickly. It will not come easily. This is where I vary from the creation story. Coming out of the darkness, chaos, and uncertainty is not as easy as steps 1 – 2 – 3. It takes time. It will probably even be a process of going back and forth between coming out and returning to the darkness and the chaos. It might even mean remaining in the darkness for some time and looking out into the light. That is okay. God is present with us whether we are in the darkness or in the light.

God is present with us and God is bringing light into our dark and chaotic world; that is the message of Christmas as well. Matthew writes that the coming Christ child is known as Emmanuel "God with us." The Gospel of John tells us that God sent Jesus into the world to be the light of the world. I am going to conclude with one more scripture.

Psalm 46:1-3, 10-11

God is our refuge and strength, a very present help in trouble. [2] Therefore we will not fear, though the earth should change, though the mountains shake in the heart of the sea; [3] though its waters roar and foam, though the mountains tremble with its tumult. Psalm 46: [10] "Be still, and know that I am God! I am exalted among the nations, I am exalted in the earth." [11] The LORD of hosts is with us; the God of Jacob is our refuge.

Sometimes the best that we can do is attempt to quiet the storms that are within us, and trust in God's presence and the coming light into our lives and our world. Amen.

December 25, 2015

Second Christmas without Ben

This is our second Christmas without Ben. In some ways, this Christmas was harder than the last. Last Christmas his death was still fairly new and emotions were still really raw. I'm not sure if the whole reality of the event had fully sunk in yet. This year the reality is much more real. We realize that the thing that we want most for Christmas will never ever happen. The flair and the glitz of Christmas has lost its shine. The excitement has lost its edge. And much of society's take on Christmas seems even more superficial and meaningless. The best that I can come back to for Christmas is "Emmanuel, God with us." There is little else to say.

This is the first year in several years that Deb and I have spent Christmas Eve and Christmas Day without any of our kids at home. Even if the older two kids were busy with work or family these past few years, we could always count on Ben being home for Christmas Eve service to help sing in the church choir and to be home on Christmas Day. The only year he wasn't home was the year that he was in Afghanistan with the National Guard unit from Mobridge. Even then we had the opportunity to Skype with him. We were able to see him, even if the picture was a little dark and fuzzy.

Lately I have been wondering, "How is it that parents who have lost children keep from going crazy?" I guess if you look through history there are some who haven't. I guess what amazes me is that any stay sane. I guess we have to simply because we have no other alternative. Somehow we have to keep moving forward. So it is that we continue to move forward into another year ...forward, still empty, still wondering...

Peace and blessings,
Pastor Keith

CHAPTER 21
ANOTHER ZINNIA STORY

January 29, 2016

Yet another zinnia story

It is the end of January. There is very little snow left in my yard. And yet, there still sitting at the end of my driveway is a dead, brown, wilted zinnia plant. I still haven't gotten the resolve to pull it up yet. It has been thirteen and a half months since Ben's death. The zinnia plant really has no connection to Ben other than the connection that I have attributed to it over the summer. And yet, as arbitrary as that connection is, I still cannot bring myself to get rid of the plant. In some ways it is almost as if while during the summer the plant was a symbol of hope and beauty to me, it has now become a symbol of my unwillingness and reluctance to let go of the pain. I …just …can't …bring myself …around to doing it. In many ways I am just kind of hoping that someday it will be gone. The plant, that is.

I know that pulling out an old dead plant does not mean I am pulling up roots and moving on without Ben. I know that getting rid of an old, dead plant is not symbolic of getting rid of all connections I had with Ben. I know that putting a dead plant in the trash does not mean that I am discarding all memories of Ben. I know that the reality is that this plant has nothing to do with Ben. I know …and yet…

I am beginning to think that that is the way it is with grief. With grief, a person does not think rationally. Grief causes a person to see things in weird ways. Grief causes a person to make strange connections between things that most people would not even consider. Grief causes a person to experience things in ways that a rational person would consider odd. A rational person would have pulled the dead plant out a long time ago.

When it comes to matters of Ben, I am not a rational person. I am still a person in grief. While I assure you that it is getting some better, I am still a person in grief.

Blessings & peace,
Pastor Keith

CHAPTER 22
BASEBALL CAPS AND YOUTHFUL INNOCENCE

February 16, 2016

Baseball caps & youthful innocence

It really isn't much. It is a simple thing really. All it is, is an orange child's baseball cap with a black "O" prominently positioned over the bill of the cap, hanging on a hook at the bottom of our basement stairs. How long it has been hanging there, I have no idea. It hasn't been worn in years. It should have been given to the Thrift Store years ago. It has only been collecting dust. But lately it has been a painful source as a reminder of days of youthful innocence and memories of playful enthusiasm. It was the baseball cap that Ben wore the two summers between his first and third grade years while we were in St. Louis while I was going to seminary. They were the Orioles.

So now this cap brings back memories of those summers of youthful innocence of an awkward little boy, whose body grew faster than his coordination, learning how to play baseball …this little boy who would with all enthusiasm play any position you put him (he liked catching the best as that gave him the most action) …this little boy who thought competitive sports were a social activity and what was for snacks after the game and being with friends was just as important as winning and losing. It is so difficult to think that this young boy who once wore this orange cap …this young boy so full of youthful innocence, playful enthusiasm, and love of life, could grow to be a young man so tormented by a mental illness that he would take his life. So difficult to understand…

But this orange baseball cap has brought something else to my realization these past couple of days. It is something I think I already knew but really couldn't explain and even now find it hard to explain. I have realized that when a parent loses a child as a young adult, (and probably at any age) they have lost more than just an adult child. They have lost more than just the hopes and the dreams that they held for that child. They have lost more than just the possibility of grandchildren. They have lost more…

They have lost the baby (that they held in their arms.)

They have lost the infant (that they used to carry and try to comfort when the child was running a high fever.)

They have lost the toddler (that they had to frantically search for who had wandered off at the state fair.)

They have lost that awkward little boy (whose body grew faster than his coordination.)

They have lost the little boy (who, in middle school, thought wrestling was a social event, not necessarily a competitive sport.)

They have lost the teenager (who they have helped to guide through high school and all of the challenges and changes that come with it.)

The list could go on and on. (Any parent who has lost a child can add their own memories and experience between the parentheses.)

An orange child's baseball cap hangs at the bottom of our basement stairs as a reminder to me that Deb and I have lost more than an adult child with hopes and dreams of a future. We have also lost the youthful innocence and the playful enthusiasm of a young boy, and so much more. The combination of the future and the past can make for a painful present. It is something that I am becoming more aware of and still attempting to learn how to live with.

Blessings & peace, Pastor Keith

April 7, 2017

The death of innocence

While preparing for their mother's funeral the daughters came across a couple of pictures from my installation service from almost seventeen years ago now. Their mother was the secretary of the Mobridge UCC church when I first came to Mobridge. The daughters thought that I should have the pictures since they were of my installation. The pictures were of everyone who had some part in the worship service which included all three of our children. Yep. There was Ben, a fourth grader at the time, standing in front with that big impish grin. And a little piece of my heart broke one more time.

Don't get me wrong. I really do appreciate the thoughtfulness of the family giving me the pictures. It is just that for some reason I am still having difficulty looking at pictures of Ben. These little pieces of mementos of happier times which should be sources of blessings and joy, two years and four months after Ben's death I still find heartbreaking and difficult to look at. I don't know if that is common for others, but it is my reality.

As I struggle through this continued process of grief, I have come to realize that what I see when I see a picture of Ben I do not just see Ben. I see the young child …the innocence …the happiness …the wonder …the curiosity …fun loving, maybe a little mischievous …loving child …all of those things that are so contradictory to the act of suicide. Thinking about this made me wonder if one of the things, among others, that makes it so difficult for a parent who has lost a child to suicide is the fact that they do not just lose a young adult child. With the death of a young adult child to suicide, a parent is also experiencing the death of the innocence of a young child. They are losing, or at least feel like they are losing that fun-loving young child of wonder and curiosity. The suicide has taken that away. And a little piece of us dies with it.

I do not know if any of this makes sense to anyone else and maybe this is not true for all parents who lose adult children. I do not know. I am just continuing to try to make sense of my experience with the death of my son.

Peace & blessings,
Pastor Keith

CHAPTER 23
WHAT DO YOU SAY?

March 30, 2016

What do you say?

Yesterday, in conversation with a gentleman about mental illness and suicide I was asked, "If you could say one thing to parents who are dealing with a child struggling with a mental illness, what would that be?"

I have to admit that I did not have a very good response to that question. I guess at this point in my life I have been too busy focusing on how to deal with the results of a mental illness when that result ends in suicide. We never knew the full extent to which our son was dealing with his mental illness. Talking about mental illness and dealing with the loss of a son from suicide is new territory for me. I'm just doing my best to muddle through and try to make sense of it all.

So it is twenty four hours later, and after much pondering I realize that I still do not have any good response. This much I would say to every parent. Love your child and support your child to the best of your ability. And let them know that you love and support them. I say this, yes, for the children who need to know that they are loved and supported. But I also say this for the parents. If you ever do end up in the unexpected situation that Deb and I have found ourselves in, you will know that you have done all that you could. You will have the reassurance that your child has known that you have always loved and supported them.

Mental illness and suicide can happen in any family, even loving, caring families with unbroken relationships. Part of what has helped to ease our journey a little is the comfort of knowing that Ben knew that he was loved and supported by his family. So to parents who are dealing with a child who is struggling with mental illness, and to all parents, I still do not know how to help or save your child, but I do know that it hurts like hell to lose one.

That might sound kind of harsh coming from a pastor, but I cannot think of a more fitting word to describe the pain.

How I wish

How I wish
For just one more
Time to see you smile
Time to hear your voice
Time to say I love you
How I wish
For just one more
Time to discuss things that matter
...thoughts about theology and God
...your hopes and plans for the future
...life
How I wish
For just one more
Time to share
...a laugh
...a hug
...a tear
How I wish
For just one more...

But who am I kidding?
The reality is...
Just one more would still never be enough.

Written by
Keith C Kraft July 24, 2015

CHAPTER 24
IT'S BEEN A YEAR AND A HALF

May 5, 2016

Ben didn't fit the mold

June 8th will be a year and a half since Ben's death. In many ways it is hard to believe it has been that long. In other ways it is almost as raw as the day it happened. Almost a year and a half …that is almost 18 months of trying to make sense of something that does not make sense. I am no closer than I was the day of Ben's suicide. Maybe I am a little biased. Maybe I am too close to the situation. But almost eighteen months have gone by and I just cannot seem to get Ben to fit into the mold of what we, or at least I, imagine for a typical suicide victim.

Ben did not grow up in a broken or abusive home. Ben did not grow up in poverty or hopelessness. As far as I know Ben did not experience any traumatic experience, whether during his military service or otherwise. Ben was not and did not experience extreme bullying. Ben was not a loner. Ben was not about to be publicly humiliated by some scandal. Ben did not exhibit extreme mood swings. Ben did not show signs of bi-polar or schizophrenia. Ben did not show signs of extreme depression or anxiety. Ben did not…

Ben was an outgoing person who loved people and loved life. And those who knew Ben genuinely seemed to love Ben. Ben simply did not fit the mold of our--at least my--understanding of one who would commit suicide. And yet, even as I say that, based on my present reality that Ben did commit suicide, he obviously did fit the mold. He was just very good at hiding it from his family, classmates, instructors, and even most of his closest friends.

Maybe what we need to do in society is re-think our understanding of the mold of those who commit suicide. Maybe, even better yet, we just break the mold and recognize that mental illness and suicide can happen in any family.

But who am I to say? After almost eighteen months, I am still just trying to make sense of something that does not make sense.

Blessings & peace
Pastor Keith

June 13, 2016

A continuing lesson in pain & loss

June 8th means that it has now been a year and half since our son Ben's death. To say the least, the past year and a half has been, "literally and figuratively," a crash course in pain education. I have been reminded that the experience and the timeline of the journey through pain are unique to each individual. The experience of pain is directly related to the relationship of the individual and the loved one who has passed away. What has been more of a learning experience for me has been the timeline for the easing of the pain …not so much the length of the timeline but as to how that timeline is determined.

At first I thought that pain was going to have to be one of those things that I was willing to let go of before it would get better. For many months I was not willing to do that. In some ways, while pain was not a welcomed friend, pain was a welcomed companion. It was, in many ways a place of comfort. It reminded me of the loss of a loved one. When love is felt, comfort is found, even in the midst of pain. Pain was also a familiar place. I knew, in the midst of my changing reality, pain would be there. It was something I could count on. So forgive me if you think I am a little bit crazy for not having the willingness to give up the pain.

But as time has progressed on this unwelcomed journey, I am developing a new theory about pain. I am beginning to think that you do not have to be willing to give up the pain in order for the pain to ease. What I am saying is that it doesn't have to be, and I would guess most of the time is not, a conscious choice. It is my experience that the easing of pain is forced on you whether you decide to let it go or not. Yes, time has something to do with it. But even more of a factor than time is that the pain becomes a burden too great to bear. The companionship of pain becomes too burdensome to carry. A person gets tired of constantly feeling the pain and little by little begins to let little pieces of it go.

Is the pain gone? By no means. The pain is still there even if it is not as sharp as it once was. It rears its ugly head in intensity from time to time, and many times at some of the oddest times and places. But little by little, and not by conscious choice, the pain begins to ease. As the pain eases, what is left in its place is a sadness attempting to fill an emptiness left by a loved one too soon gone.

Blessings & peace,
Pastor Keith

CHAPTER 25
ANGER AND GRIEF

September 18, 2016

Anger and grief

Twenty and a half months since Ben's death and I still have not experienced the anger. Those who know say that there are different stages of grief that people experience after the death of a loved one, one of which is anger. I even had someone last spring tell me that I needed to experience and express the anger if I was going to move through the grief process. Sorry, I still have not experienced the anger …at least not the deep intense anger usually associated with the unexpected death of a child by suicide.

The past two weeks have almost been "suicide" overload for me personally as I have worked with a family through a funeral of a suicide victim combined with several conversations with others on the topic of suicide. Several people have been concerned and have asked me how I am doing because of the funeral. My answer has always been "ok." Probably a more honest answer would be, "numb." It's hard to explain. I'm not feeling much of anything other than compassion for the family for their loss. As for me there is not overwhelming sadness. I didn't feel like I was going to "crash" during the service or at any time. I just felt numb. It's not about me and a person does what has to be done. I would like to think it was my professionalism, but I sometimes wonder if it is just another way of God protecting me from the reality.

But still no anger. Over the past two weeks I have witnessed the anger that others have experienced. With the anger has come the blame. In some ways I feel cheated. I have nothing and no one to be angry with or to blame. There are many times that I would like to have something or someone to blame because then it would help to make sense of this senseless death. But I can't. I cannot blame the army or his experience in Afghanistan. I cannot blame bullying. It wasn't drug or alcohol abuse. Ben was not experiencing humiliation or shame. Ben didn't come from a broken family. Ben had his whole future ahead of him. Ben had friends. Ben loved life. Ben had a loving and stable family life. There is no reason that Ben should not be alive …at least in my mind and my reasoning.

So the only thing that I am left to be angry at and to blame is this illusive thing that we call mental illness …this thing that no one can really see or explain, and some might even question its validity. The difficult thing is that Ben made it even more difficult because he kept his anxiety and depression so well hidden from us that it is even hard to say with confidence that that was the issue. But it is the only thing that makes any sense at all.

But it is because I have nothing else to blame that I have the courage and the determination to continue to speak concerning mental illness and suicide. I do not wish to become an annoying parent with a cause, but I need to speak for I know there are those whose experience is similar to ours. Another reason I speak is because every person who has experienced the loss of a loved one from suicide needs to know that he or she is not alone.

In the meantime, I am still waiting for the anger stage of the grief process. Maybe I have experienced it and don't really know it. Maybe my anger has been reserved for people who have tried to over simplify the cause of suicide or put the blame on the victim. Anyway after these past two weeks I can hear Semmi Gond Kabin calling. But that too will have to wait.

Blessings and peace,
Pastor Keith

There are days

There are days I wish I had permission to throw a big ol′ temper tantrum.

I wish I could just stomp around, yell, scream, throw things, break things

…maybe even kick something.

There are days that I wish that I had permission to just be sad

…that tears would flow on command

…that people could see a broken heart.

And then there are days that I wish I could just feel nothing at all

…that I could just sit and feel

…nothing

…no pain

…no sadness

…no grief

…no

…nothing.

Some days they all come in one day.

Written by
Keith C Kraft February 3, 2017

CHAPTER 26
DEATH BEFORE AGING

November 11, 2016

Death before aging

With the coming of Ben's second birthday since his death I am even more aware that the only thing that can stop the progression of time, is death. Death is the only thing that will stop the aging process …at least in our minds. I say that because our son Ben will forever be 24 years old. Deb made that comment several months back. I had never really thought about it, but it has rattled around in my brain ever since. I realize how true that statement is. And I also realize how wrong that statement is. It is just wrong that death comes before aging. Parents should have the ability to watch their children grow older …maybe even have children of their own if they so choose.

Ever twenty-four

To your mother and me
You will always be
Ten days plus year twenty-four
That was your age
When you last turned the page
Not one day or one year more

It just doesn't seem right
That you lost the fight
To the darkness that dwelled in your mind
Or that our lives go on
With your unfinished song
And the peace that we struggle to find

Our comfort and peace
In your sweet release
Is only found in God's healing power
And knowing nothing could erase
God's all-encompassing grace
Present with you in your darkest hour
Keith C Kraft November 28, 2016

CHAPTER 27
THE TATTOO

November 26, 2016

Semicolon tattoo

So I just did something that at one time I swore I would never do. I got a tattoo. While Ben might not have been shocked with this, he would have been surprised. I'm pretty sure he knew that I was never overly thrilled with his tattoos.

But this is more than just a tattoo. It is a tattoo with a very personal meaning to me. I suppose that most tattoos have significant meaning to those who get them. But this is personal for me. I got a semicolon tattoo with the inscription Genesis 1:1-2. I struggle some with the idea of getting a tattoo, but the reality is that the tattoo is an outward sign of an inward reality. The reality is that our son Ben's death has left a permanent mark of pain tattooed in our heart. I will guarantee you that the pain in my arm will long subside before the one in my heart.

The semicolon comes from the concept of the Semicolon Project. The semicolon is a symbol for those who are struggling with thoughts of suicide or for family members who have been touched by suicide.

Similar to a semicolon in a sentence which is placed where there could be a period but instead a semicolon is used and the sentence continues on, the semicolon represents the fact that a person's story continues. The stories of those who struggle with mental illness and the families who have lost loved ones to suicide must be told and they must be told without shame or humiliation. The stories must be told without shame or humiliation or the mental illnesses will continue to be hidden and family members of suicide victims will continue to experience the isolation of the stigma that goes with it. A semicolon represents a person's willingness to share the story of how suicide and mental illness has touched his or her life.

For me personally death might have ended our son Ben's life, but his story continues on in his parents, siblings, and friends. I will gladly and without shame share his story and my experience to anyone who would like to hear it. I want family members of other suicide victims to know that they are not alone and that suicide is not a sign of mental weakness in their loved one any more than losing a family member to cancer is a sign of physical weakness. Suicide is a mental illness that needs to be talked about to help eliminate the shame and the stigma that goes with it. This tattoo is, at least I hope, a conversation starter.

The Genesis text is a comforting reminder to me that the same God who was present in the darkness, chaos and uncertainty in the beginning of time is the same God who was present with our son in his darkest hour in the time leading up to and at the time of his death. That same God continues with us in our times of emptiness and uncertainty.

Peace and blessings,
Pastor Keith

The tattooing experience/ (connecting with Ben)

February 1, 2017

For over two months now I have been debating whether I should write about my tattooing experience or not. Even as I begin to write this I am still hesitant to share it. It is not because I find this deeply personal. As most of you know by now, when it comes to Ben's death and suicide I am more than willing to share. No. What makes me hesitant is that I know that once something is put down in print and shared publicly the writer has lost all control over how it is understood. It is really up to the individual reader as to interpretation and understanding. So please understand that what I write is strictly a sharing of my experience and nothing more. I am not promoting or justifying any type of activity. This is just me and pain continuing to seek understanding. I will leave it at that.

If you have read my blogs before, you know that this past fall I got a semi colon tattoo to continue the story of my son Ben. My tattoo artist knew my purpose and understanding of my reason. During the process of getting the tattoo I mentioned that Ben had three or four tattoos. Without missing a beat my tattoo artist asked if Ben "cut". I replied that I honestly did not know, but that a friend of Ben's suggested that he possibly had. Again, without missing a beat the tattoo artist commented that it is not uncommon for people who cut to get tattoos.

For those of us who have never experienced the inner pain and torment of a mental illness, we can only wonder and surmise at the reasons for cutting. To purposely cause one's self physical pain does not make sense. I had always thought perhaps the reason for the cutting was to cause one's self physical pain so as to take one's mind off the inner pain. Maybe it is for some. I do not know.

But my tattooing experience opened for me another possibility. At one point as I was going through the pain of the tattoo process an odd sensation came over me. It is really hard for me explain or describe in either printed or spoken word. It was as if, at least for a little while, that my skin had been cut open and some of the inner pain was being released. There was a sense of release and relief ...at least for a little while. Again, it is hard to explain. The best way I can explain is that in some ways it was like poking a hole in a throbbing blister and the relief that comes when then the infection starts to ooze out.

It was at that moment that I began to wonder if that is why Ben did it. If Ben did cut, did he cut as a way to release some of the inner pain that he was dealing with? Is that why Ben got tattoos? Did Ben experience that same release of inner pain? Were the times that he got tattoos times that he was feeling the pain of the darkness closing in on him?

I will never know. Only Ben could answer those questions. I only know that there was a moment during my tattooing experiences I felt a connection and a little deeper understanding of my son Ben. It was enough to bring a tear to my eye …not from the physical pain, but from the release of a little bit of the inner pain and the connection to my son that I felt.

For that connection and possible understanding, I will always be thankful.

Blessings and peace,
Pastor Keith

CHAPTER 28
TWO YEAR ANNIVERSARY

December 7, 2016

Two year anniversary

Just a humble "Thank You," to members of the church, friends, family and to all of you for your support and prayers for Deb and me and the family over the past two years. A special "thank you" to the church for your patience as I struggle to find my footing.

Wishing you all continued…

Blessings and peace,
Pastor Keith

Two years

It's been two years,
You've yet to come home
I miss you as much now
As the day you left.
If it is possible,
I miss you more.
Confirmed by the pit in my stomach
And the pain in my chest

I know why
You have not been home
But the passing of time
Makes it that much more real
Real as the love
That creates a special bond
It is that special bond
That makes it difficult to heal

But this I reassure you;
You are never
Far from my thoughts
You are always in my heart.
In that way you are
always here with me
And we have never,
Never ...ever
been apart.

Keith C Kraft December 7, 2016

CHAPTER 29
CONTINUING TO SEEK ANSWERS

February 16, 2017

"Is suicide a choice?"

Okay, so I apologize for more ramblings concerning suicide but there is just something (actually many things, but one thing in particular) that has really been bothering me lately. I have heard several times since Ben's suicide that family members should not feel guilty about their loved one's death because it was their loved one's choice to commit suicide. I agree with this statement to a point. There may be several reasons to feel guilty, but the cause of the suicide is not one of them. A person might feel guilty of hurtful words said or words left unsaid or something such as that, but not the cause. The person and the person alone chose to commit suicide.

But there is where I have a problem. Is suicide really a choice or has something inside the brain taken away that choice from the person? I ask this question based on my own experience of knowing my son. I truly believe that at any other given time other than when Ben's mental illness dragged him down into that deep darkness that he experienced Ben would have chosen life, not death. I truly believe that Ben wanted to live but there was something in his mind that took him to a place where he was robbed of that choice.

I might be completely off base in my thinking here. I have no way of really knowing. I am simply going off of my personal experience with my son. But if I am correct or at least even partially correct I wish that there was a better way to say it than to say that someone chose suicide. Some might think I am splitting hairs here or even wonder if it makes a difference.

As a father of a son who committed suicide, it does make a difference to me. To say that a person who commits suicide has a choice makes it sound like someone just decided to check out of this life because he or she did not like the way things were going or did not like the other options. It over trivializes the reality of the situation and somehow puts it into the same category of someone trying to make the choice of going to college or a trade school or going right into the work force. It makes the suicide victim sound selfish or weak because they "chose" the easy way out.

Is suicide really a choice? Some might argue that it is a choice. Some might argue that in some cases it really is not a choice. Possibly.

Yes, my son chose to commit suicide in that no one else influenced that decision. But if one's mind takes a person to a dark and painful place where one's judgment can only reason that the only way out is suicide, is that really a choice? Just wondering.

Blessings & peace, Pastor Keith

February 21, 2017

Seeking answers

An unnerving thought just crept into my mind. In my search for understanding of my son's death by suicide, do I really want to know the answers? Or is it possible that I only want to know the answers that agree with what I think or what I want to believe? To learn the truth or possible truths is a frightening thing. We might learn hidden truths about our loved ones that are unsettling.

I am finding that in the search for understanding I am also finding out some things about myself as well. I am finding that I want things the way that I want things. I want to believe what I want to believe and I tend to resist different understandings …at least at first. I want to make sense of this thing that we call suicide but I want it to make sense in the way that I think or believe. I am stubborn. I am resistant. I do not like to change. Unfortunately or fortunately, when seeking understanding, change is inevitable and sometimes one has to be unsettled by truth to eventually find peace in understanding.

CHAPTER 30
PARENTAL CONCERNS

June 18, 2017

Father's Day the Third

It is Father's Day and I wore my bright pink dress shirt to church this morning. It might seem odd to wear pink for Father's Day and probably more appropriate for Mother's Day. One of the things that I learned from my son Ben is that it is "okay" to be a little odd and to break tradition once in a while as long as you are true to yourself. I wear my bright pink shirt on those days when Ben is even a little more on my mind than usual. Father's Day is one of those days.

This is now our third Father's Day since Ben's death from suicide. It is a day when I think of Ben a little more and again I am reminded about how much I miss him. One of the things that has always concerned me through this grieving process is that I hope that my other two children do not feel lost or abandoned in the process. I hope that they do not feel that my love for them has somehow been diminished because of the pain and love expressed over the loss of Ben. I'm not very good at expressing love the way it is, even when the love is there.

I can understand how a parent can get so wrapped up and overwhelmed with the grief from the loss of a child that the other children might feel neglected. They might wonder where they fit in to larger scheme of a parent's love. When praise is given to the child who has died, the other children might begin to question, "Where is my praise? Am I as appreciated as the child who has died?" They might begin to question, "Am I loved as much as my sibling who is no longer with us?"

I hope my children have never wondered or questioned those things, but I do understand how they could when I continue to blog about thoughts on Ben and his death. As a parent who has lost a child, it can become a challenge to balance the pain and attention given to the child who has died with love and attention given to the children still living. So to my children I say, "I love you both very much and I consider you God's greatest gift and blessings to me …outside of your mother, of course. Thank you for your patience and your love for a grieving parent. It is something I should have said, but something I hope you know even if it is not spoken."

To the rest of you who might read this, hug those you love for they truly are God's greatest gift and blessings.

Blessings and peace,
Pastor Keith

November 11,2017

Blessing and a curse

There is something that has been somewhat bothering me since Ben's death. I was reminded of it again the other day through a short visit I had with a mother who has just discovered that her two young adult daughters have a rare form of cancer. I can only imagine what it must be like for the parents of these two children …the constant worry …the frantic concern …the sense of desperation …the sense of helplessness. I can only imagine that there must be this constant nagging in the pit of the stomach that never seems to go away. I can only imagine the sleepless nights of worry ...wondering about an uncertain future. I can only imagine.

I can only imagine because we did not have that with Ben because we did not know. I sometimes wonder how I would have handled things if I would have known. We knew somewhat that Ben was dealing with some or at least had dealt with some mental issues, but we did not know to what extent. We were never fully aware to what extent Ben suffered from mental illness of depression and anxiety. He never shared that with us. Because Ben never shared that with us we never really experienced the constant worry of when were we going to receive that phone call that said Ben had died by suicide. We never had that sense of desperation of whether or not there was viable treatment out there for Ben. We never had the sleepless nights wondering if Ben was safe or not. We never had... We never had because Ben never shared his illness or let us know. Ben was very good at hiding the seriousness of his disease from us and others.

As I have experienced it, this not knowing (to borrow a phrase from the television series, Monk) has been a blessing and a curse. Yes, we did not have the constant worry, the sleepless nights, the feeling of desperation and helplessness. But we also did not have the opportunities. We did not have the opportunity to help or offer guidance. We did not have the opportunity to encourage Ben to seek treatment or help him seek out treatment. We did not have the opportunity to let Ben know how much we loved and cared for him in spite of his illness. We did not have the opportunity to let Ben know that we accepted him in his illness. We did not have the opportunity to work with Ben in the hope of finding healing and wholeness. We did not...

Do not misunderstand me. I am not the least bit envious of these parents or any parents who face the challenges of their child dealing with a serious illness. I am just saying that knowing and not knowing come with different and unique challenges. So which is preferred? ...knowing your child is seriously ill and experiencing the helplessness, worry and anxiety that go with the journey? ...or avoiding the stress of the journey because you did not know, receiving a visit from the police informing you your child has died, and wondering how things might have been had you had the opportunity? My preference would be "neither." My preference would be healthy adult children. But it is not to be. So we just have to figure out a way to continue to move forward with the challenges life gives us whether it is "knowing" or "not knowing."

My heart truly goes out to the young ladies and their parents. They are truly special people. I hope they whip this thing that we call cancer. I do not and cannot know what the young ladies or their parents are going through right now. I can only imagine and I am guessing that what I imagine might not even be close. I can only say my thoughts and my prayers are with them. To them and to all of you I truly wish you all…

Blessings & peace,
Pastor Keith

CHAPTER 31
ANOTHER LOOK AT ANGER AND GRIEF

August 13, 2017

Another look at anger and grief

A couple of months ago I was visiting with a lady who had lost her husband to suicide when she was a young mother with young children. She told me that she was very angry with her husband for taking his own life. She suggested that maybe I did not experience the same anger because of my son's age. Ben was younger than was her husband at the time of their respective deaths.

This thought bothered me. Shouldn't my loss give me the right to be as angry as anyone else who has lost a loved one? Age shouldn't be a determining factor. In some ways, don't I have the right to be even angrier because my son did not have the opportunity to live as long and experience things in life as others do? Shouldn't I have the right to be angrier because I have been deprived of more time and experiences with my son?

After some thought I began to wonder if maybe this lady was right …to an extent. Maybe she was right, but I wonder if it was not age that made the difference but the relationship. As a young parent, I too would have been very angry to have been left alone to raise children that two of us had brought into this world. I would have been angry that my spouse would have singlehandedly destroyed the hopes and dreams of a life that we had planned together.

But it was not my spouse who committed suicide. It was my son. As a parent, I am supposed to raise and protect my children. It gives me great sadness to realize that I could not protect my child from the darkness that drove him to suicide. Yes, I am angry with the situation, but it is a situation that was beyond my control. The darkness of the mental illness made it a situation that was beyond my son's control. I am not angry with Ben. For me, it is the sadness that over shadows the anger.

In one of my earlier writings I mentioned that pain is relational …dependent on the individual and the loved one who is lost. The reality is that the whole grieving process is relational. No one can judge or determine where another might be in their journey through grief. Grief, and how we experience it is both individual and relational.

Blessings & peace,
Pastor Keith

January 10, 2018

Grieving as a pastor

The road through the grief process is filled with challenges. That is a universal truth. Each individual's journey through the grief process is unique based on the individual and the individual's relationship to the one who has died. That is another universal truth. It cannot be said that any certain person's journey is more difficult or challenging than someone else's journey. With that being said, I can only speak or write on my own personal experience as a pastor and as a father whose son died by suicide. Both bring with them their own challenges.

As a pastor, one's grief is public. There is no way around it. There is no way that one can just go off and shut one's self off from the world and grieve in private. Each week when the pastor steps into the pulpit the pastor carries the baggage of grief with him or her. Each day, as public figures that represent God and their church, pastors carry that grief with them when they meet people out in the public. In my case, (good, bad, or indifferent) I will always be known as the pastor whose son died by suicide. This is especially true in a small town where everyone knows almost everyone. They for sure know who the pastors are in town.

Since the pastor's grief is public there is the pressure or challenge of modeling healthy grieving …if there is such a thing. In grief, one's vulnerability is on display. Pain, sadness, anger, confusion …a whole mix of emotions come boiling to the surface. The challenge for the pastor is to determine how much of those emotions does one express? Members of the church and the community want to know that their pastor is vulnerable. They want to know that their pastor hurts, feels pain and sadness, and deals with all of the same challenges of the grieving process as they do.

The members of the church also want to be reassured that their pastor is not "losing it." Other people can "lose it" in their personal grief, but a pastor cannot. A pastor has to deal with the grief of others so they had better know how to handle their own grief and have their grief under control. If pastors cannot deal with their own grief, how can they deal with mine? Since loss and grief are so much a part of life, the pastor feels that it is his or her responsibility to the church and to the public to model healthy grieving. The challenge for the pastor then becomes how to balance vulnerability with strength? That balance must be on display, at least in the public …in which they are most of the time.

Whether this understanding is real or just perceived by the pastor, it is still the pastor's reality. It is the one within which he or she lives.

Blessings and peace,
Pastor Keith

CHAPTER 32
WHAT'S IN A WORD?

August 21, 2017

What's in a word?

After my last reflections writing a week ago I received an email from a parent who lost her son to suicide after a long battle with depression and anxiety. In her email she suggested that I no longer use the word "committed" suicide and instead use the term "completed" suicide. Her reasoning was that "committed" gives the connotation that the person committed a crime, which they didn't. Her email got me to thinking about words and terms we use, how they are perceived, and where did they first come from.

First of all, let me say two things. One, thanks for the email. I appreciate comments and insights on things that I might not think about. Secondly, my writings are meant in no way to offend anyone especially anyone who is already dealing with the loss of a loved one from suicide.

As I said, her email got me to thinking. "Committed" is the only term I have ever heard when referring to death from suicide. It is ingrained in my head. I wonder if the term "committed" didn't first become used because (I think) at one point suicide was considered a crime …albeit, a crime against one's self. A quick google search shows that suicide has been decriminalized in most countries but "failed attempt suicides" in some countries can still be considered a felony.

So if "committed" gives the false implication that one has committed a crime, what then is a better word or term? Another quick google search and I came across an article titled "Language about Suicide (Part1): The Power of Words written by Stacey

Freedenthal, PhD, LCSW. http://www.speakingofsuicide.com/2013/04/13/language/ Dr. Freedenthal suggests that both words "committed" and "completed" are insufficient. Dr. Freedenthal suggests that instead to use the phrase "died by." You can read Dr. Freedenthal's article by clicking on the link above. At the risk of misquoting it, I will let the article speak for itself.

For some the discussion on an appropriate word to use might seem like overkill on political correctness. For me it is trying to be sensitive to those who are already dealing with the pain of a loss of a loved one. That is important. Personally, "died by suicide" seems to be most appropriate and it is the term I will attempt to use from now on. My son died from a mental illness of depression and anxiety. His death was by suicide.

I realize that old habits, especially old habits that are so engrained in my psyche are sometimes hard to break. Again, thanks to the one who sent me the email. Any time we can share thoughts and raise awareness around mental illness and suicide, it is a good thing.

Blessings & peace,
Pastor Keith

December 20, 2017

The question of a "merry" Christmas

"Merry Christmas" or "Happy Holidays"? For some the debate continues as to which is the proper "Christmas/holiday" greeting. For many, this debate is moot because they really do not care. For many others, there is no debate. There is no debate because the Christmas holiday season is neither "merry" nor "happy." There are many who struggle to find the joy in what has become for most a joyous time of the year. Knowing that others are feeling the joy and you are not, makes the struggle with this time of year even more difficult. It makes one wonder if he or she is odd or the Christmas Scrooge or Grinch because others are expecting you to feel the same joy and holiday spirit that they are.

I remember stating at our son Ben's funeral three years ago that for me and my family there will be no joy this Christmas. Maybe in the future, joy would once again return. This will be the fourth Christmas and the joy has yet to return. While many of you might find that sad, quite honestly, I am "okay" with that. I am "quite comfortable with not feeling the Christmas spirit that most other people do. Joy is not the only message of Jesus coming into our world.

Luke is the only Gospel that refers to joy at the time of Jesus' birth and that joy is mostly reserved for the lowly, the forgotten, and the marginalized. The Gospel of Matthew is the only other Gospel that records a birth story of Jesus and his message is twofold: he will save his people from their sins and Emmanuel, "God is with us." It is a message for the all peoples. There is no birth story in the Gospel of Mark where the message of the coming of Jesus is to turn back to God. Again, there is no birth story in the Gospel of John where the message of the coming of Jesus is God's light coming into a darkened world.

The underlying and deeper message in all four Gospels is the message of hope. Joy is sometimes fleeting at best, many times circumstantial, and often reserved for a privileged few. Hope is universal and eternal. No matter our circumstances, we can all use hope. Without hope, there is no joy.

So no matter your circumstances this Christmas holiday season, whether this is the "happiest time of the year" for you, or you are still grieving the loss of a loved one, or you are experiencing depression and anxiety or you are stressed out from the pressures of the holiday season--no matter where you are in your life's journey-- in Christmas there is always a message of hope for all of us. There is hope that God reaches out to be in relationship with us. There is hope that God's presence is with us. There is hope that we have not been forgotten. There is hope of God's light shining in the darkness of our lives and our world.

It is "okay" if there is no "merry" in your Christmas or "happy" in your holidays. There is always hope for you, your life, and our world as witnessed through Jesus coming into our world. Wishing you a blessed Christmas.

Blessings and peace,
Pastor Keith

CHAPTER 33
HELLO SADNESS

October 12, 2017

Hello sadness

Hello Sadness my old friend
I've come to talk with you again

Yes, I know that I changed the second word of Simon and Garfunkel's hit song, "Sound of Silence." As I continue through the journey of grief now well into its third year, it just seemed fitting. It seems that sadness is and will be a lifelong companion on this journey through life. It seems that sadness is and will always be a part of my mental and emotional psyche. I say this based not only on my own experience but also from what I have witnessed in others who have lost loved ones, especially those who have lost a child or a spouse.

I have noticed as of late that the sadness has also showed up in my sleep. I would not call the dreams nightmares. The dreams are not terrifying or unsettling in any way. The word I would use if there was such a word would be "sadmare." They are dreams about Ben or hints of Ben and yet deep down, even in my dream I know that Ben is gone. It does not happen often and in fact only a couple of times that I remember. Dare I admit it? I have even cried a couple of times in my sleep.

I do not mean for this writing to be some type of killjoy or downer. It is not a ploy for sympathy. It is just an observation of the experience. Sure, there are many times of happiness and even times of joy. Time with my children and grandchildren is always special and they bring me happiness and joy. There are many other times as well when I am doing things I enjoy or experiencing some sense of accomplishment that there is a sense of happiness. But it seems that there is a sense of sadness that is always dwelling underneath it all. It is like it is just sitting there waiting to surface. It is usually in those times of quiet and silence that it is most prominent, but it is also present when I am in the midst of people.

So the sadness remains. In many ways it is like an old friend on a lifelong journey. I know it will probably always be there. I also know that for the rest of you, three years probably seems like a long time ago. You are probably wondering what is taking so long for me to get back to normal. Like it or not, this is my new normal. So do not expect me to be happy all of the time. Do not ask me to smile or move on. Respect my sadness. Accept my times of sadness and the fact that it is and probably always will be a part of who I am. I have. And I'm okay with that. It may sound weird, but sometimes being sad makes me happy in some odd way. So you do not know. Maybe when I am sad, I am also happy.

Blessings & peace,
Pastor Keith

Sadness my friend

Sadness comes
like a welcomed friend
As I sit in the silence
trying to comprehend
The loss of a child
with so much hope
Yet struggling with a darkness
which he could not cope

The grief from that loss
must continue on
And with that grief,
sadness tags along
He comes on strongest
when all is silent
He continues to linger
even when the tears are spent

But that's okay,
do not feel sorry for me
For it is in my sadness
that grief is set free
At least for me,
in matters of grief
In the silence and the sadness
I experience some release

For I trust in a God
of great compassion and care
Who, through the journey of grief,
is already there
So if you see me in my sadness,
just smile and nod
For you know that it is then
that I am closer to God

written by Keith C Kraft July 31, 2018

"God is our refuge, and strength, a very present help in trouble. Therefore we will not fear though the earth should change, though the mountains shake in the heart of the sea; though the waters roar and foam, though the mountains tremble with its tumult.
Be still and know that I am God!" Psalm 46:1-3, 10a NRSV

CHAPTER 34
GOOD FRIDAY MESSAGE

March 31, 2018

Good Friday to Easter

Mark 15:34 "My God, my God, why have you forsaken me?"

The Gospel of Mark records these words as spoken by Jesus as he hung on the cross. In these nine words you can hear the anguish of one who is experiencing pain, both physical and emotional. You can sense the desperation and forsakenness of one who feels abandoned. You can feel the hopelessness of one who feels the agony of separation from the one he loves.

This Holy Week, as I continue to think about my son and his death by suicide, I have wondered if he felt much the same. I wonder if he didn't, in his own way, feel the pain and the anguish of separation …not a separation necessarily from God, but a separation from loved ones and the world. This feeling of separation was imagined, brought on by the mental illness of depression and anxiety which made it very real to him. It would be enough to make one feel forsaken, abandoned, alone, and hopeless. I wonder if that is what he felt. I wonder if that is what pushed him to the act of suicide. I wonder…

The message of Easter and the Resurrection is that God had not forsaken Jesus. The continued message of Easter and the Resurrection is that God has not and will not abandon us. In life and in death, God is present. That is our promise and our hope for our loved ones who have died. That is our promise and that gives us hope as we continue to learn to live in reality of that separation brought on by death and all of the challenges that come with it.

March 30, 2018

Good Friday Hope

Even in the midst of
the bleakness,
the emptiness,
and the darkness;
God is present.

CHAPTER 35
THEY JUST DON'T UNDERSTAND

July 26, 2018

They just don't understand

Another suicide in our community and my heart cannot help but grieve. I did not know the young man, but my wife knew him from school. He was an intelligent and ambitious young man; valedictorian of his class, working three jobs, enlisted in the South Dakota National Guard. He was trying to make things work. I grieve for him, for his family, for his friends, for our community, and for the world in general. Another young life taken too early. Who knows what contributions he might have made to our world and the difference he might have made in the lives of others. I grieve his loss ...our loss.

A common phrase I have heard from older adults throughout my life at times of a suicide, especially when that suicide is a young person is, "These young people just do not understand. Death is a permanent solution to a temporary problem." This statement is made assuming that the suicide is the response to a temporary crisis in a person's life. I understand this thinking as I have thought it before. Even in my mind, I struggle with that thinking with my son. Ben knew better. Ben was smarter than that. Ben was smart enough to know that death is permanent and crises are circumstantial and temporary.

It is when I get to the point of asking in despair, "Why Ben? You knew better. You were smarter than that." It is then that I have to say, "Yes, Ben knew better." Ben's act of suicide was not the actions of a young man who was thinking rationally. We assume that a person who takes his or her own life by suicide is thinking (for lack of a better word) "normally." Ben knew better. I would guess that most people who take their life by suicide know better in those times when mental illness is not controlling their thoughts and actions.

Again, I insert the disclaimer that I am not a trained psychologist. I am not educated in the field of brain disorders and mental illness. I am still trying to make sense of mental illness and suicide almost four years after our son's death by suicide. I am simply going off of my own experience of Ben and others, as well some things I have read. It is my experience of Ben and others that those with mental illness whose lives end in suicide really do not want to die. That might sound like an odd statement as it is the person who dies by suicide who takes his or her own life. My experience of my son was that what he wanted most was to live a life just like everyone else ...a life free of the depression and the anxiety ...a life free of the darkness. They really do want to live. It is when the darkness becomes so all consuming that the brain does not function as it should. Reasoning is gone.

This much I do know. We need to quit assuming that the act of suicide by a young person is somehow an irresponsible childish act by someone who should know better. They do know better when mental illness is not in control.

The reality is, it is us who do not understand. The best thing we can do is to first admit that we do not understand and will never fully understand. We can then move from that acknowledgement to then not passing judgment. We do not understand therefore we should not try to pass judgment on the actions of that we do not understand. From there we move to compassion, not pity. A family does not need pity. They need compassion. They need support in their loss …support in the way that they need it, not in the way we might want to give it. Let our support be on their terms to meet their needs.

My heart grieves…

Blessings & peace,
Pastor Keith

CHAPTER 36
DARK FAMILY SECRETS

August 5, 2018

Dark family secrets

Our granddaughter who is almost three spent the night with us the other night. She did not bring any of her toys with her as she assured her mother that grandma had toys. Besides her pajamas the only thing she brought with her to sleep with was her blanket. Before she went to bed our granddaughter picked out a stuffed big bird to take to sleep with her. It was our son Ben's big bird that he used to sleep with when he was about that age.

Our granddaughter never knew her uncle Ben. We were blessed with her presence into our lives some ten months after Ben's death. Our granddaughter might not have ever known her uncle Ben, but I do know that I want her to know about him. I want her to know about Ben, and I want her to know how he died. I do not want Ben and Ben's death to become like some deep, dark family secret that the family tries to hide. I know of families who do not talk about "Aunt So and so" who was a little "crazy," or never really knew how "Uncle So and so" died because the family just did not talk about them or the way they died. They were embarrassed and thought that it brought shame to the family.

I will always be proud of Ben and I will never be ashamed of him or the way he died. I do not want Ben's nieces and nephew to be ashamed of him or his death either. A disclaimer before I go any further on the topic of discussing suicide/mental illness with children: I am not a trained child psychologist or counselor. My thoughts are simply my personal thoughts based on personal experience. Please, do not be afraid or ashamed to seek professional help in sharing such a difficult topic with your children or grandchildren, especially if the person who died by suicide was a close relative to the children such as a parent or grandparent. Your child's emotional and mental health are important.

With that being said, the family members who are left behind play an important role in a child's understanding of that individual's death as well as suicide and mental illness. The challenge is that there are at least three issues of sharing such a difficult topic of suicide with children: when, how, and what. When or at what age do you start to talk to your children or grandchildren about mental illness and suicide when the topic is related to a family member? How do you bring up or approach the topic of mental illness and suicide? And how much and what do you tell your children or grandchildren?

To these questions, I do not have the answers. I am not sure anyone has the answers. When, how, and what to share about mental illness and suicide is so individual. It depends on the child as to when they are ready to hear about such a difficult topic and how much they can comprehend at the time. A person does not want to traumatize a child. We do not want to give them unnecessary nightmares or bad dreams. We do not want to overburden a child with too much "heavy" information or emotions.

Naturally, the best time is when the child is ready. Hopefully, a parent or grandparent will have a sense of when the child is at the age that they are ready to hear the realities of mental illness and suicide. The best way to discuss such a topic would be naturally and not forced. Children are often inquisitive. They might ask, "How did grandpa, or dad, or aunt or uncle die?" If they are ready to hear the truth, share it with them. How much to share and what to share is another question. The important thing is to approach the topic from a factual standpoint and not an emotional one. The reality is that when it comes to the topic of suicide and mental illness each family will have to muddle through and figure out when, how, and what is best for each child.

The main thing when sharing with a child about the death of a family member by suicide is to be open, honest, and unashamed. Children quickly pick up when an adult is uncomfortable about a topic or ashamed of the results. If they sense that the adult family member is ashamed and uncomfortable with a topic, they will take on that attitude for themselves. On the other hand, a person needs to be sure not to glorify the person or the act when discussing the topic of suicide with children or youth. Young minds are easily impressionable and some things can be misinterpreted.

Children learn primarily from their parents and grandparents and guardians. If we are open, honest, and unashamed to talk about mental illness and suicide, maybe we can pass that same attitude on to our children. Maybe then mental illness will not be so hidden and suicide will not carry the stigma for families that it does.

At least for me, I want my grandchildren to know about their uncle Ben. I am not ashamed of him or his death and I do not want them to be either.

Blessings and peace,
Pastor Keith

CHAPTER 37
THE CABIN

July 29, 2018

The cabin

Deb and I have a little piece of property with a cabin in the southern Black Hills. We purchased this piece of property with the plan to eventually build for retirement. We were mainly looking for property on which we could build at a later time. The cabin is an extra bonus as it happened to be on a piece of property that fit what we were looking for. With our daughter living in Rapid City, South Dakota, and our son living in Denver, Colorado, we felt that the southern Black Hills was a good option for retirement. Deb and I have always enjoyed the southern Black Hills. It is a place where I personally can feel and experience a spiritual connection with God. In my opinion, our Native brothers and sisters got it right. There is something spiritual about the Black Hills. The cabin has been a gift to me and to us since Ben's death. But there are times I feel guilty about having the cabin and this peaceful retreat.

The times of guilt are there because the reality is that we most likely would not have this property with this cabin if it had not been for Ben's death. The topic of where we would retire never really came up before Ben's death. Where to live when we retired was a topic to be discussed in the future when retirement was closer. We only knew that in our retirement we would like to live within some proximity of our children. With Ben still going to school we had no idea where he might end up living. Our other two children are pretty well settled with where they are living. It was only after Ben's death that we started looking or even thinking about purchasing property with the possibility for our retirement. Without Ben's death we would have waited and this piece of property would not have been available. So there are times when I feel like this nice place of peaceful retreat has come at the cost of our son's life.

Okay, so I know that is a piece of irrational thinking, but it is mine. But I also know that this property has a deeper meaning because of Ben's death. It has been a place for a peaceful retreat when things start to get a little overwhelming. It is also a place where I can come and do some physical work. It is surprising what good emotional and mental therapy a person can receive in cutting trees. It is hard to explain, but it has been a rewarding activity for me this sabbatical. Cutting trees requires some thinking as to how to cut a tree down so that you do not hurt yourself, but other than that it is mostly physical work. At the end of the day a person can tell that he or she has done something.

So the cabin has been a place where I can come and retreat when things get a little overwhelming. It is a place where I can come and sit in the silence and continue to process the loss of our son. Sometimes in the silence the sadness comes on a little stronger. That is okay. I can sit in my own sadness. I can grieve in my own personal time and space without distraction. But the cabin is also a place where doing some physical work can be a welcomed distraction. It is not emotionally, physically, mentally, or spiritually healthy for a person to be in a constant state of sadness and grief. The cabin has become a space for me for both: a place to privately grieve and a place for distraction from the grief. A person should not need to feel guilty for sanity. In some ways the cabin has helped to preserve mine.

The cabin has become one of my ways of processing and continuing through the grief process. The time and space are important for me. The same is necessary for others who have lost a loved one with whom they were very close. They need both time and space to continue to grieve. In many ways, all of us, even those who are not in the middle of the grieving process could use a little personal time and space for their emotional, mental, and spiritual health.

Personal time and space are precious gifts in our busy, sometimes crowded world. The cabin has been and continues to be mine. For you who are reading this, I hope you find yours …whatever and wherever that might be for you. When you do find it, you do not need to feel guilty about taking advantage of it. There should be no guilt in emotional, mental, and spiritual well-being.

Blessings & peace,
Pastor Keith

CHAPTER 38
REFLECTIONS AFTER FOUR YEARS

July 17, 2018

Reflections after almost four years

We are steadily approaching the fourth anniversary of our son Ben's death from suicide. There are still images, sounds, and experiences that run through my head as if it were yesterday: the phone ringing at five in the morning, my wife Deb crying, my heart sinking. I can still hear my other two children's sobs of disbelief. It was on that day that we first learned that our daughter was pregnant with her first child. I remember feeling robbed …cheated out of the joy that should have been from hearing our daughter was pregnant with her first child. I also felt guilty for taking the joy from her of sharing that news.

Someone once told me that when God takes a loved one out of the world, God sends another to take his or her place. This thinking brought no comfort to me in the loss of our son. I wanted my son alive. Besides, I do not believe that God takes people out of the world through death. Death is a part of being human and mortal.

After hearing the news of Ben's death my sister Nancy told me, "You have just become a member of a club you never want to be a member of, but you will be for the rest of your life …a parent who has lost a child." That comment I can verify as truth. Nancy and her husband would know too. They lost a daughter about the same age as Ben two years earlier.

Much has changed in our lives since Ben's death. The journey through grief has been, well, a journey through grief. It has been a journey of pain, emptiness, and sadness. In reflecting back over the past almost four years now it would be easy to get stuck there. It would be easy to get stuck on reflecting on the pain, emptiness, and sadness of the grief process. But the reality is that there have been some good things ...many good things that have happened as a result of the grief process as well.

For one, I have a greater awareness of mental illness and suicide. I cannot say that I have gained any greater understanding of mental illness or suicide. Personally, whether it is true or not I do not know, but I have become more convinced of the connection between the two. It is sad that it took the death of my son to make that connection. There are many different types and severities of mental illnesses. Not all mental illnesses lead to suicide, but I would venture to surmise that most suicides are the result of a mental illness. I am still trying to increase my understanding of both.

I told myself at the time of Ben's death that I did not want to be a "parent with a cause." But I also think it is important to raise awareness, understanding, and support for individuals with mental illness and their families, and the loved ones left behind in the event of a suicide. Since Ben's death we (those of us who have been touched by suicide and mental illness) have started a Mental Illness/Suicide Yearly Awareness (MISYA) event. The event consists of a walk, some type of education and awareness, and a brunch. We have also started a Suicide/Mental Illness family support group that meets once a month. During Christmas we have a longest night service for anyone who might be struggling to find the "merry" in Merry Christmas.

These are positive things, not only for me but also for our community, that have come about as a result of Ben's death by suicide. The rise of these things gives me a greater understanding of John 12:23-24 [23] *Jesus answered them, "The hour has come for the Son of Man to be glorified.* [24] *Very truly, I tell you, unless a grain of wheat falls into the earth and dies, it remains just a single grain; but if it dies, it bears much fruit."* It is not that God wanted or caused Ben's death so that these things would happen. It is just that these things grew as a result of Ben's death. It is our hope that by raising awareness and understanding maybe some other family will not have to experience what we have experienced.

The other thing that I have come even more aware of as I reflect back on my journey through grief so far is that there were many good people who have helped me along the way. From Ben's army sergeant and the police officer that had the difficult task of bringing us the news of Ben's death, to the funeral home directors and my interim conference minister who helped prepare for the funeral, there are so many people whom I have gained a greater appreciation for through this journey. I have not journeyed through this grief process so far in isolation.

My church and individuals of my church have been supportive and patient with me. I know it was a shock to the church just as it was to us and many of them did not know quite how to react around Deb and me nor did they know what to say. The comments I appreciated the most at the time of Ben's death were from those who said, “I just don’t know what to say.” It was perfect …heart felt and honest. I know these past four years have not been easy for our church family but I hope they know I appreciate their support and patience. If I tried to name them all I know I would leave out someone.

Besides my church the other smaller group of people who have been helpful on my grief journey has been our mental illness/suicide support group. Currently, it is a small group of only four to six of us. We get together once a month. Sometimes we talk about mental illness and suicide. Sometimes we talk about what is going on in our lives or the lives of our families. Sometimes we just talk about who knows what. The important thing is that we share a commonality which is our bond. We have all lost a family member to suicide.

There are three people that I do think are important for me to mention. One is Pastor Paul. Pastor Paul is a colleague serving another church in Mobridge. Pastor Paul also lost a son a few years before our son's death. The circumstances of his son's death were different than my son's death. The two important things that we have in common are that we are both pastors and we have both lost a son. I found myself in his office several times. I appreciate our chats which have helped me process the challenges of both being a pastor and unexpectedly losing a child.

Another person that I really appreciated and continue to appreciate through this grieving process is the person who works with me almost every day. Misti is our church office administrator and my colleague in the church office. She has supported me and has allowed me to be me through this whole grieving process. Misti has tried to protect me and my space when I have needed it …one time, even physically blocking the way of someone who wanted to see me as I was preparing for Ben’s funeral. She understood that it was not a good time for visitors. Misti also understood the significance of the oddly placed zinnia and helped to protect it as well. She made sure that someone put a bucket over the zinnia when he sprayed the rest of my yard for weeds. It might seem like a simple thing but it meant a lot to me. For some people, “thank you” will never fully express the appreciation that is felt.

The person that I appreciate the most is the one who lives with me and has to put up with me every day ...my wife Deb. There is no one …no one I would have wanted to go through this loss and grief process with other than Deb. Many times, the death of a child can pretty much destroy a marriage relationship. I can understand that. Both parents are trying to deal with their own pain and grief. It is difficult to support a spouse when you are crashing yourself. Then there are those times …many times when the two of you are in two different places in the grief process. It is not easy grieving together as parents. There are days I wonder how or why she put up with me through the process. But there has never been a day that I have wondered if our love would see us through. I know that we have a long way to go through this loss and grief process …a lifetime to go, but with the strength of love that we share and a faith and hope in God, we will go through it together.

I share all of this for a couple of reasons. One is to let those who might find themselves in a similar situation, struggling with the unexpected loss of a loved one, know that they do not have to journey through the grief process alone. I am not generally a "support group" type of person, but I have found our small group very helpful. Find an individual you trust who might try to understand what you are experiencing. Find a church or an organization with which you connect. Share your story of loss. Raise awareness. Seek understanding. Find what works for you that helps you with the healing process.

For me, the healing process continues. Much has changed since our son's death. The biggest change is that we have three more grandchildren. They will never take the place of Ben but they have been a great blessing to aid in the healing process. The difficult part is knowing that Ben would have adored them all. While much has changed, one thing has not. There is still and will always be a big hole in my heart and an emptiness in my life that only Ben could fill. It is not to be.

So how am I doing almost four years after Ben's death? Much of that depends on the day. If it is possible, my children and my family have become more important and precious to me. Times spent with them are precious and not often enough. I don't think my kids know quite how to handle Dad's emotions in his greetings when they come and his saying good-bye when they leave. I worry a lot more about my children than I used to. With Ben's mental illness, I hesitate to say this but I worry about my grandchildren and their mental health.

There is one feeling that comes over me from time to time that has surprised me. There are times that I feel proud of myself. Maybe I should feel ashamed for saying that, but I do not. I am proud that I have made it this far on the journey of grief since Ben's death. I have not gone into deep depression. My marriage is still intact and going strong. I still have a job and I can still function at that job. That is pretty good. Anyone who can still function after the death of a child or a spouse has a right to be proud.

I still find it difficult to look at Ben's pictures. My emotions are still very close to the surface. I experience sadness quite often. There are times, for some reason out of the blue the thought of the method of Ben's death will come to mind and it will about bring me to my knees. It breaks my heart to see little children, especially little boys, cry. I have a new grandson, Martin Bennett. I am really wondering what my relationship will be like with him. I'm afraid Grandpa might get a few tears quite often over the little guy. (But being a man, I will attempt to keep those times private.)

Of course, it goes without saying that I miss Ben a lot. There are many days that I still cannot believe this has happened. I still find it difficult to believe, much less understand why Ben took his life by suicide. The act of suicide just does not match the boy and the young man that I knew. Ben loved life. Ben loved people. I have yet to make sense of something that does not make sense. Otherwise, I'm doing as well as can be expected.

All in all, I do not think I am doing too badly. A therapist might have other thoughts. Anyway, these are just some thoughts that have been going through my mind lately as I continue to try to process Ben's death.

Blessings & peace,
Pastor Keith

CHAPTER 39
SUICIDE AND HOPE

July 11, 2018

Suicide and hope

Suicide is the act of total hopelessness …at least that is the prevailing thought. It makes sense. After all, who would choose death over life if there was any hope at all? As Jurgen Moltmann points out in his book Theology of Hope, hope is open to a realm of possibilities. *"Hope alone takes seriously the possibilities with which all reality is fraught. It does not take things as they stand or lie, but as progressing, moving things with possibilities of change."*[2] In other words, hope is open to a future with the possibilities of change. Only a person who understood that there was no possibility of change would choose to not live into that future. So we might draw the conclusion that when it comes to suicide, mental illness robs an individual of hope.

But there is another aspect of hope that we have to consider. Hope will also cause one to act. If I have hope for a different future than what I am currently experiencing, I am going to work towards that future. If I do nothing to attempt to bring about that changed future then it is only wishful thinking. In that respect then, is it possible that suicide is an act of hope? Could we rationalize that a person who chooses to take his or her own life is acting in the hope of taking away the pain or the total despair that he or she is currently experiencing? This person is hoping for something better. He or she is hoping for some type of relief …any type of relief…hoping for some type of better future than they are currently experiencing. If the person had no hope that things would be better or that the act of suicide would take away the pain and despair, he or she would do nothing and would simply wish it would all go away and thus remain in the current state of pain and despair.

Let me insert a disclaimer here. I will readily admit that I do not understand suicide or mental illness. I do not know what is going through the mind of one who chooses to take his or her own life. I am only trying to make sense of something that I do not understand and I am trying to make sense of that through my own experience and that of my son who died by suicide. My understanding of mental illness and suicide is a work in progress.

With that being said, I wonder if, oddly and sadly, suicide is an act of hope. Is suicide an act of hope in the midst of total hopelessness? The problem is that the mental illness has taken away all possibilities of hope but one …death. Hope opens the future up to a realm of possibilities. Mental illness can take a person to a place of such darkness and despair that all she or he sees is one possibility of hope for relief …death. Is it possible that that one possibility of relief is what moves a person to action ...to take his or her own life? All other options are gone. Or is it that dark and chaotic feeling of total hopelessness ...that feeling that there is absolutely no possibility of change that moves a person to action ...to take his or her own life?

I am just raising the question as a possibility. Most people would argue the latter, that suicide is an act brought about by the feeling of total hopelessness. One thing is for sure. Suicide is an irrational act so trying to make rational sense of it is really irrational. The reality is that it really does not matter whether suicide is an act done out of one desperate act of hope to relieve the pain or an act brought about by total hopelessness. Either way, the results are the same. A valuable life is lost. Hope or lack of hope is still the issue. Suicide is an act brought about by the severe loss of hope that takes a person to a dark place that most of us would never understand.

It is important for us to recognize and acknowledge that that absence of hope in the midst of deep darkness is the reality of some people. As loved ones, friends, and as people of compassion we should be asking, "How can we change that reality? How can we help someone begin to see and understand that hope brings with it a whole realm of possibilities ...positive possibilities?" As a Christian and as a pastor, I must ask, "What hope do we as the Church and as Christians have to offer ...not only for those who are suffering mental illness, but also for those who have lost a loved one to mental illness through suicide, and for our society as a whole?"

Blessings and peace,
Pastor Keith

CHAPTER 40
HOPE AND HEALING

July 18, 2018

Hope and healing

Acts 3:1-10

"One day Peter and John were going up to the temple at the hour of prayer, at three o'clock in the afternoon. 2 And a man lame from birth was being carried in. People would lay him daily at the gate of the temple called the Beautiful Gate so that he could ask for alms from those entering the temple. 3 When he saw Peter and John about to go into the temple, he asked them for alms. 4 Peter looked intently at him, as did John, and said, "Look at us." 5 And he fixed his attention on them, expecting to receive something from them. 6 But Peter said, "I have no silver or gold, but what I have I give you; in the name of Jesus Christ of Nazareth,[a] stand up and walk." 7 And he took him by the right hand and raised him up; and immediately his feet and ankles were made strong. 8 Jumping up, he stood and began to walk, and he entered the temple with them, walking and leaping and praising God. 9 All the people saw him walking and praising God, 10 and they recognized him as the one who used to sit and ask for alms at the Beautiful Gate of the temple; and they were filled with wonder and amazement at what had happened to him." **Acts 3:1-10** (NRSV)

I would venture to guess that most of us, if not all of us, at one time or another had one of those "aha" moments. Usually it comes at a time when a person is not expecting it. Many times the "aha" experience is over something that you have seen or experienced many times before. The difference is that this time life circumstances are different and your mind is in a different place. Something that you have seen many times before "hits" you differently and it is like a light comes on. Your eyes are opened in a new way. This thing has been before you all of this time and it makes you wonder why you have never seen it or understood it this way before. A parishioner of mine called those experiences "when God winks."

Such is my experience with Acts 3:1-10. Acts 3:1-10 is just another healing story in our scriptures. It gives evidence that what once was the ability to heal that Jesus had, has now been given to his disciples to carry on his mission and ministry. A man lame from birth can now walk as a result of the healing ability of God through Peter (who represents the Church) given to him through his faith in the resurrected Christ. Not only can the man walk, he can run and jump. This is not a small feat given that fact that the man has never walked before in his life.

This is a very familiar text. I remember singing a song in Sunday school based on this song. "Gold and silver have I none, but what I have I give to you. In the name of Jesus stand up and walk. And the man went jumping and leaping and praising God." …something to that effect.

This scripture was used as part of a Bible study for the staff of the Hungarian Reformed church in Abaujvar, Hungary. Unexpectedly, I heard this very familiar text with new understanding. Unexpectedly, I heard this story, not only as a healing story, but also as a hope story. Think about it. Here is a man born lame. He can do virtually nothing for himself. His whole life he has relied on the goodness and the kindness of others. He has to wait for someone to carry him to the gate of the temple where all he can do is beg from others. He relies on the kindness of others to drop a few coins in his cup so he can have a little to provide for himself.

The man born lame has never stood eye level with anyone else. He has always had to look up to others. Or another way of putting it: everyone else looks down on him …literally and for many people probably figuratively as well. Most people probably saw him as just another beggar wanting some of their hard-earned money.

The man born lame had little hope. I'm guessing he had no hope of healing as he never asks for it. He only asks for alms …just enough money to make it through another day. What hope the man had was placed in the kindness of others.

Then one day, unexpectedly, without even asking, everything changed. A man heals him in the name of Jesus Christ. Suddenly, he can do something he has never done before in his life. He can walk. Not only can he walk, he can run and leap! He is healed! This is fantastic! Now, not only does the man born lame experience healing, he also experiences hope. There is hope for something better. There is hope beyond begging for subsistence every day. There is hope beyond just hoping on the kindness and goodness of others. There is hope in the healing that now he can provide for himself.

There is also some apprehension that comes with the healing. This man born lame has never worked a day in his life. All he knows is begging. He has no life skills or trade skills. The disciples just took away his one means of living …begging. But still there is hope for something better. There is hope for something better because not only did the disciples heal the man born lame, they restored his faith and his relationship with God. "The man born lame was leaping and praising God." It is a relationship restored. With a relationship with God, there is always hope. It is in our relationship with God that we find our hope.

My "aha" moment was that I realized, or maybe was reminded of, how intricately related are hope and healing. Healing brings hope. There is hope in healing when healed a person can do things that he or she could not do when he or she was sick or crippled. But as any doctor or cancer patient will tell you, hope is also a very necessary aspect of healing. Hope is what keeps a patient pressing forward towards healing. Hope is what keeps doctors and researchers looking for better cures. Hope is sometimes the only thing that will keep a patient going through treatment and enduring the pain that comes with the treatment. There has to be hope for a cure or at least some type of remission or an individual will just give up. Hope and healing are intricately woven when it comes to illnesses.

The difficulty of hope is when the illness is a mental illness. A mental illness robs a person of that hope or it says that death is the only way to end the pain. The challenge for mental illness is to somehow keep the hope alive …somehow broaden the person's understanding of hope. It is a challenge. It is a fight. Sometimes, too many times, it is a fight that we do not win.

But it is a fight that we must continue. We must continue to better understand mental illness. We must encourage and support research to find a better understanding of mental illness and seek cures for those who suffer from mental illness. We must keep the hope alive that both understanding and a cure or at least help is possible.

As the Church there is little that we can do on the medical front in offering physical or mental healing. Unless you are a medical doctor, most of us do not have that ability. But we do have the ability, as the Church, to help others restore their relationship with God. But in order for us to help others restore their relationship with God we have to be and to act like the Church, the body of Christ. We have to act in loving ways to each other and to others. We have to be welcoming and non-judgmental of those with mental illness. We have to be supportive of those who have lost loved ones to suicide as a result of mental illness. In other words, we have to act Christ-like to others if we are going to have any hope of helping others heal their relationship with God.

Hope and healing: they go together. As always, hoping that healing will bring…

Blessings and peace,
Pastor Keith

CHAPTER 41
SALVATION AND HOPE

August 2, 2018

Salvation and hope

Within two weeks of our son Ben's death to suicide I received a letter in the mail with an article in it. The article was written by someone who had done an interview with former NFL coach Tony Dungy. In this article Tony talked about the death of his son by suicide. He stated that he found comfort in knowing that his son had accepted Jesus Christ as his Lord and Savior and that he now had salvation in heaven with God. This part of the article was highlighted for me. I assumed the attempt was that the person sending me the article thought I would find comfort in knowing the same; that my son had salvation with God in heaven.

While the well–meaning attempt was to bring me some sense of comfort, it did not. I am a selfish father. I did not want my son in heaven. I wanted my son with me. God did not need my son as much as I did. God does not need us. We need God. And yet, so much of the hope that we speak of in the Church is a salvation hope. Sometimes it seems that, to Christians, it is all about what happens after we die. To those outside of the Church, the only hope we offer is a salvation hope …and that hope only involves heaven …a peaceful pleasant place to go after we die.

While that might have been some of what Jesus and the early church was referring to when they talked about salvation and being saved, I sometimes wonder if we, as Christians and in the Church are missing the point. From my limited understanding of Greek from several years ago in seminary, the word which salvation is translated from finds its roots in the Greek word "sozo." It is the same word that Jesus uses when he tells people that their faith "has made them well." With "sozo" comes the sense of healing or wholeness. Being saved or finding salvation isn't just about where you are going after this life is over. Salvation and being saved is about experiencing healing and wholeness right here, right now.

What good is it if the only hope we offer those who are suffering from mental illness, and the pain and the darkness of depression that comes with it, is the hope of a pleasant peaceful life with God after their deaths? Why wouldn't they want to "check out" of this life if the only hope we, in the Church, have to offer is a life free of pain with God after death? What comfort are we really offering to loved ones after the death from suicide is if the best we can offer is a hope that their loved one rests with God, when all they really want is their loved one with them? As a parent who has lost a child to suicide, I can honestly say, "very little." Three and a half years after Ben's death it gives some comfort, but at the time of his death, it was not what I wanted to hear.

Maybe we as Christians and we in the Church need to spend less time focusing on and talking about salvation as a death retirement plan and "being saved" as whether you have your premium paid in full. Maybe we need to focus on salvation and "being saved" in the here and now. Maybe we need to rethink salvation and "being saved" in the terms of wholeness and healing for today.

As I watched my mom die from cancer some thirty years ago, I witnessed that healing can come without a physical healing. Healing can come from knowing that God is present through it all no matter what the circumstances are. Wholeness comes from experiencing the love, grace, and presence of God no matter where you are, what you are dealing with, or what you are going through.

Only God can offer and bring salvation when it comes to matters of what happens after death. We have nothing to do about that. It is only through the grace of God that we are saved. But when it comes to matters of salvation of wholeness and healing, we do have something to offer. We can offer the same love and compassion that God has shown us. We can be the presence of God in our care and concern for others. We can be Christ's body in the world today.

We, in the Church and as Christians, need to go beyond the trite responses of just telling those who are suffering from depression and mental illness that they need to just pray about it …(with faith that is). Or telling those who have lost a loved one to suicide that their loved one has found salvation in heaven. Those words are meaningless and hollow as words.

What those who are experiencing mental illness and those who have lost a loved to suicide need are words with actions …actions that say, "I really do care." Actions that say, "God is present with you and to show you that that is true, I'll do my best to be the presence of God for you right now." Actions that say, "I know you are broken in your mental illness or in your sorrow, but I will not turn you away or ignore you." Actions that say, "You are important to me, because you are important to God." Actions that say, "Come and experience the healing power of God's love and presence …I will walk with you until you do." Maybe that sounds trite as well, but when it comes to attempting to heal brokenness, actions go much farther than words.

Don't get me wrong. I do find some comfort in the hope and faith that Ben has found rest in God's eternal care. I live with the hope and the faith that Ben has found peace from the turmoil and darkness that the mental illness tormented him within his life. The hope of salvation in God's love that we offer in the Church to those who have experienced the death of a loved one is an important task of the Church. Sharing the salvation hope of rest in God is an important way that we in the Church can encourage one another at the time of a death.

But there needs to be more when the emptiness is great. There needs to be more when the only hope is to end the pain through death. There needs to be the experience of salvation this side of death. Most of us do not have the power or the ability to bring mental and physical healing. But all of us have the power and the ability to offer the healing power of God's love and compassion through acts of compassion and responding in love.

Blessings & peace,
Pastor Keith

CHAPTER 42
THE CHURCH AND HOPE

July 17, 2018

The Church and hope

"These three remain: faith, hope, and love and the greatest of these is love," is what Apostle Paul writes to the Corinthian church, 1Corinthians 13:13. Faith, hope, and love are the three pillar essentials of our faith. Without any of the three, our faith is pretty much dead or stagnant, which is not much better than dead. It was my hope that when it comes to matters of dealing with people with mental illness or those who have lost a loved one from mental illness through suicide that one of the things the Church had to give is "hope." Even as fluid, futuristic, and intangible as it is, at least hope would be something. I would rather have something concrete …something tangible to give someone …something that they could hold on to that would make their life better. Hope is at least something.

Lately I have been a little bit envious of doctors and the medical profession. People who are ill walk into a medical facility, see a doctor for their illness, and walk out with some type of prescription for treatment in their hands. It is visible. It is concrete. It is tangible. It gives each person hope of getting better. Even when the illness could possibly be terminal like cancer. "Here are the odds but with the advancements in treatments those odds are getting better." The person might walk out of that office still uncertain about the future and maybe even scared to death, but there is hope in her or his hands.

The Church is not like a medical facility. The Church does not have a written prescription to give hope that it might take away the darkness of mental illness. The Church does not have a pill that might give hope to ease the pain of the loss from suicide. We cannot say, "Do these things and your mental illness will go away or the pain of your loss will ease. To experience hope you need to pray and read the scriptures daily. Oh yeah, and be sure you pray with faith that you will be healed." If that is what we are giving people with mental illness or the loss of loved ones, we need to really reconsider our prescription of hope.

The reality is that we really have nothing to give that could possibly instill hope. We in the Church cannot give hope, but just as important, we can offer hope. We can offer hope by pointing to the God of promises in which we place our hope.

The whole of our Bible is based on hope from the beginning to the end. In the beginning God created the heavens and the earth out of nothing in hopes of something very good. God created humankind in God's own image in hopes that humankind would take care of this wonderful creation. Sin enters the human picture bringing about a separation of the relationship between humankind and God, a separation in the relationships within humankind, and a separation in the relationship between humankind and creation. God attempts again and again to reach out to humankind in the hopes of bringing humankind back into right relationships.

Abraham is promised a land and many descendants. He and Sarah leave their homeland in hopes of realizing that promise. The Israelites are promised freedom and a land. They find their exodus from Egypt in hopes of realizing that promise. The exiles of Israel hope to return to their homeland. There is the hope of a promised Messiah. Jesus raises the hopes in some that he is the promised Messiah. Jesus demonstrates that the hope of salvation does not come from the land or the Law but through a personal relationship with God. Our hope lies in re-establishing a relationship with God

Jesus' death and resurrection brings hope that sin and death do not have the final word. There is hope in life …hope in new life in Jesus Christ. There is hope in the coming of Christ's reign on earth where all things will be put in right order. There is the hope of a new heaven and a new earth, not by destroying the old, but as

Apostle Paul points out in Romans chapter eight, "birthing out of the old."

As the Church and as Christians, we place our hope in the God of promises who kept God's promises in the past. God kept God's promises to Abraham, and Isaac, and Jacob. God fulfilled God's promises to the Israelites and brought them into the Promised Land. God brought the people back out of exile. God sent a Messiah in Jesus Christ. God has always remained faithful in keeping God's promises. These past promises and the faithfulness of God give us hope for the promise of Christ's future reign and the world being in right relationship with God …a world where there is no more pain and sorrow, and every tear shall be wiped away.

God's faithfulness in promises kept in the past gives us hope for the present. God promises God's love and presence throughout our lives. God was present in the beginning. "In the beginning when God created the heavens and the earth, the earth was a formless void and darkness covered the face of the deep, while the wind (spirit) of God swept over the face of the waters." Genesis 1:1-2. Even in the darkness and chaos, God was and is present. God is present in the darkness of mental illness. God is present in the chaos of our lives following the unexpected death of a loved one by suicide. God is present working to bring order to our sometimes dark and chaotic lives.

Not only is God present with us. God knows us intimately. Apostle Paul tells us in Romans 8:26 and 27 that the Spirit intercedes for us in sighs too deep for human words and God who searches the heart knows the thoughts of the Spirit.

"[26] *Likewise the Spirit helps us in our weakness; for we do not know how to pray as we ought, but that very Spirit intercedes with sighs too deep for words.* [27] *And God who searches the heart, knows what is the mind of the Spirit, because the Spirit intercedes for the saints according to the will of God.*" **Romans 8:26-27** (NRSV).

My first year at Eden Seminary in St. Louis I was placed at Deaconess Manor as a student chaplain. One of the residents that I frequently stopped to see was a lady who had a bone disease that made her bones so brittle she was completely bedridden. It took four people to gently move her from her bed to rolling reclining chair. During one of my visits she asked me to write a prayer for comfort for her. In my search and struggle to come up with a prayer I happened to come across Romans 8:26 -27. These verses gave her some peace of mind. It was a comfort to her that, not only did God know her pain, God felt and experienced her pain with sighs too deep for human words. This is our hope as Christians.

In an interview with Michael Moore in September of 2017 Jim Carrey shared his thoughts on the power of hopelessness. Yes. You read that correctly. Jim Carrey reveals that he has embraced the idea of giving up on hope when confronted with tough times. He says that you do not have to worry if you give up on hope. Whatever will be, will be. You do not have the stress of worrying about hoping things will get better and then being disappointed when they don't. It is freeing.

It might be freeing, but it does not change our reality. Resigning oneself to hopelessness does not change a thing or help to change the lives of others. Hope at least gives a person something to work for ...something to strive for ...a reason to live and move on. The difference for those of us in the Church and those of faith is that we place our hope in the one in which we place our faith ...God. We do not place our hope in the actions of people. People too often let us down and disappoint us. God is faithful and it is the faithfulness of God that we place our hope.

The challenge with any hope is that it is long term. It is for something in the future. Again, as Apostle Paul writes in **Romans 8:24-25**, (NRSV) "[24] *For in hope we were saved. Now hope that is seen is not hope. For who hopes for what is seen?* [25] *But if we hope for what we do not see, we wait for it with patience.*"

We cannot see it. We do not hope for something that we are currently holding in our hands or currently experiencing. Hope is futuristic. Many times what is hoped for is in the distant unknown, uncertain future. Hoping for something in the unknown, uncertain future requires patience. But it also requires more than just patience. Hope needs something to sustain it through the struggles and challenges of life. Our hope as Christians is sustained through faith. Hope and faith are intricately woven together. Our hope is a product of our faith. Hope gives our faith meaning. Faith sustains our hope into the unknown, uncertain future.

In order for hope and faith to be possible there needs to be something credible in which to place that hope and faith. As Christians our hope and faith are placed in a God who has made and kept promises. The faithfulness of God is centered on God's love for us and for the world. Our hope and our faith are placed in the love of God. It is a love that, as Apostle Paul goes on to say in **Romans 8:39**; (NRSV) "*there is nothing that can separate us from that love; not death nor life, nor angels, nor rulers, nor powers, nor depths, nor heights nor anything else in all creation.*" I would add: nor mental illness, nor despair, nor depression, nor anxiety, nor hopelessness, nor grief can separate us from the love of God. For those of us who have lost loved ones to mental illness and suicide, that is our hope in which we place our faith.

Like hope, we cannot give anyone faith. Faith has to come from within the individual and from one's own personal experience of God. As the Church and as Christians we can share our faith. We can point to the God of our faith and hope. We can also offer to walk in faith and hope with those who need to experience a sense of hope as they continue to journey through their struggles. Through walking together, we can grow in faith and hope together. While we as Christians and the Church cannot give hope, we can offer hope. We can offer hope by pointing to the God of our hope and faith.

We can also be instruments of hope. We become instruments of hope through offering ourselves in love. The Church and we as Christians can offer ourselves in love. We can offer ourselves in love by not turning our backs on those who are experiencing mental illness or those who have lost a loved one to suicide. We can offer ourselves by graciously reaching out to those who are struggling with the darkness and the chaos. We can offer ourselves in love by offering to walk with them ...encouraging those who are seeking treatment ...supporting those who have lost loved ones. Sometimes ...many times the greatest love we can offer is just silently being there and letting those who are struggling with a mental illness or the loss of a loved one know that we are there for them. Letting them know that we care. In short, it is called the ministry of presence. When we look beyond ourselves and offer ourselves to others we can become instruments of hope.

The love that we live towards those who are experiencing mental illness and those who have lost loved ones to suicide is how we point to the God of our faith and hope. That is the story of Jesus Christ. Jesus' actions and preaching were not about "Jesus." Everything that Jesus did was about God. All the miracles that Jesus did and compassion that Jesus displayed, pointed to God. Through our nonjudgmental acceptance of those with mental illness and our compassion shown towards those who have lost loved ones to suicide, we too can point to a God of grace and acceptance much the same way Jesus did.

When we are instruments of hope through welcome and acceptance we can also become a place of healing. The Church is called to be a safe place of healing for the broken in our world. The Church is at its best when it lives and reaches out in the love of God as lived out in Jesus Christ.

Through the Church and as Christians we can offer hope and healing. We offer hope by pointing to God and the faithfulness of God in which we place our hope. We also offer hope through our love lived in the faith of the God of love and grace. Through acts of welcome, acceptance, and compassion we become instruments of healing.

Blessings & peace,
Pastor Keith

CHAPTER 43
MY HOPE AND HEALING

July 29, 2018

My hope and healing

I carry a scar. I will carry this scar for the rest of my life. Actually, I carry two scars that I will carry for the rest of my life. One scar is visible that I carry on my right arm. The scar is in the form of a tattoo. This scar is a result of another scar that no one can see. No one can see this scar because I carry it within me. I carry within me the pain of the loss of our son from suicide. The scar that I carry on my arm is a direct result of the scar of the pain that I carry within me. I had never even considered getting a tattoo until after our son's death. The scar on my arm is an outward sign of an inward reality of the scar of pain that I will always carry.

The scar on my arm is a tattoo with a semicolon followed by "Genesis 1:1-2." The semicolon is a reminder to me that our son Ben's story continues. I will continue to carry Ben's story with me for the rest of my life. The semicolon is also a symbol that I have been personally touched by suicide and that I am willing to share my story and my son's story. The reference to the scripture verses Genesis 1:1-2 is because in my search of hope and healing that is the text to which I keep circling back.

Genesis 1:1-2 (NRSV) *"In the beginning when God created the heavens and the earth,* 2 *the earth was a formless void and darkness covered the face of the deep, while a wind from God swept over the face of the waters."*

It is from this tattoo that I find my strength. It is a continual reminder of God's presence that was with Ben in his most dark and chaotic time at the time of his death. It is also a continual reminder of God's presence with me throughout this journey through grief and pain, and throughout the rest of my life. So, this tattoo is a constant reminder of the One in whom I place my hope. It is a reminder of my faith.

I remember one of my Old Testament professors in seminary suggesting that the first creation story was probably written at a time when the Israelite peoples were in exile. The time of exile was a dark and uncertain time for the Israelite people. The creation story gave the people hope that the same God who brought light and order to a dark and chaotic world in the beginning (day one …day two …day three …day four…) could bring light and order to their uncertain world.

In many ways I would like to have light and order back in my life. Slowly, it is coming. But with the death of our son from suicide, I am not sure that it is ever fully possible. The title of a parent who has lost a child to suicide will always be a part of who I am. I will carry the pain and the sadness of that loss for the rest of my life. Never fully understanding that loss is something that I will also carry. The odd thing is, as much as I would like to get to the light and have the order in my life, I am really in no hurry to get there. It is okay to linger in the darkness, chaos, and uncertainty. There is really no need to hurry through the grieving process. I am "okay" with where I am. God is present in our darkness, chaos, uncertainty, pain, sadness, and grief. In many ways, God is closer than we could ever imagine.

Knowing the faithfulness and the presence of God is where I find and experience my hope. It is that hope that has helped and continues to help me move through the healing process of the loss of my son. It is also my hope that my son Ben is okay. It is my hope that Ben is now free of the darkness and the pain that tormented him in this life. It is my hope that Ben is now at peace resting in God's care. I would love to know for sure that Ben is okay. I trust that he is, but I do not know for sure. So, it is that for now I cling to hope.

Reflecting back on the healing process that I have experienced so far on the journey through grief, I have come to realize that much of the healing also circles back to the beginning …the creation story …the second creation story in Genesis.

Genesis 2:18, 22-23 (NRSV) [18] *Then the LORD God said, "It is not good that the man should be alone; I will make him a helper as his partner."* [22] *And the rib that the LORD God had taken from the man he made into a woman and brought her to the man.* [23] *Then the man said, "This at last is bone of my bones and flesh of my flesh; this one shall be called Woman, for out of Man this one was taken."*

This creation story in Genesis is more than just about a man and a woman coming together in marriage. It is more than just a story about procreation. This Genesis story is about who we are as human beings. God created us as relational human beings. "It is not good that the man (or woman) should be alone. I will make him (or her) a helper." God created us relational. We not only share common flesh and bone; we also share common experiences. Through our shared experiences we can help and support one another through the difficult challenges we face in life.

God has always called a people. God called the people of Israel. God might call an individual to do a specific task, but it is always the people that God is calling. Jesus did not call just one disciple. Jesus called several disciples together. God calls us as a church community. It is within this community that we not only worship together, but also find our support and care. We are the care givers and the care receivers. It is not good for man or woman to journey through the difficult times in life alone. God gave us a helper or helpers. It is the way that God created us.

I have not moved through the healing process this far in isolation. My wife Deb has been a very important part of the healing process. Even though we have not always been in the same place in our grieving, we have always found support in one another. We have found strength in one another. Communication has been very important to the grieving process together. We have been able to share our anger, our grief, our pain, and our sadness with one another. As a man, sometimes that sharing can be difficult. After all, society tells us that men are supposed to be the strong ones in the relationship and women, the emotional ones. There is strength in vulnerability when expressed in a loving relationship. God could not have blessed me with a better partner/helper to journey with through this tragic experience.

The church has been an important aspect of my healing process as well. They have supported Deb and me from the very beginning. So many members of the church have expressed their concern about how we are doing. Some have expressed their concern verbally. Some have expressed their concern through actions. Either way, I felt it and I knew it was always there. Their concern for our well-being has been a great comfort and support to both of us through this difficult time. The death of a pastor's son to suicide has been a new and unwelcomed experience, not only for Deb and me, but for the church as well. In many ways we had to learn together. I appreciate their patience with me as we have worked through this grieving process together.

The other group of people who have been an important aspect of my healing process is our Suicide/Mental Illness Family Support group. We organized and met for the first time about nine months after Ben's death. It is a small group of only four to six of us who meet on a monthly basis. Sometimes we talk about our pain and grief from the loss caused by suicide. Sometimes we talk about what we are going through at that particular time. Sometimes we talk about family. Sometimes we just talk about nothing in particular. It is a space where we are free to share, cry, and laugh. We know that those in the room will understand. Our experiences might vary a little, but what is important is that we are there together and that we share a common experience ...the loss of a loved one from suicide. Just knowing that someone else knows some of the challenges we are facing is comforting and supporting.

Never underestimate the healing power that can be experienced in the support of others. Typically, I am not a support group type of person. I would rather figure things out on my own.

But there is healing in sharing our stories. There is also healing in listening to the stories of others. Also, do not underestimate the importance of participating in a support group even if you do not feel it is necessary for you personally. It is very helpful and healing for others to hear the stories of those who have already been on the journey of grief for a while. There is hope when listening to the stories of others who have "made it" as far down the journey as they have. It gives hope to others that they too will "make it" through the grief.

Through a hope and faith in God and the support of family, the church, and many others there has been healing. It does not mean that life is all back to normal now. It is the hope, faith, and support that are helping me move into my new normal without Ben. I do not expect the healing will ever be complete, but I do expect that with a hope and faith in a God of compassion and the love and support of so many others, that the healing will continue.

I am reminded of a country song by Gary Allan, "*Life ain't always beautiful.*" [3] Life is not always beautiful. There will be pain. There will be tears. Life is not always beautiful, but it is a beautiful ride.

Sometimes, in the midst of the loss, pain, and grief it is hard to experience that beautiful ride. Sometimes in the sadness you wonder if you will ever experience the joy again. But the reality is, life is a beautiful ride. We can experience God in the grief and the loss. We can grow through the pain. We learn to appreciate the gifts of love in the support and compassion of family and friends. We treasure time spent with loved ones a little more.

I know the journey through grief of the loss of my son will be a lifelong journey. But I am still on that journey and that gives me hope.

As always, wishing you continued…

Blessings & peace,
Pastor Keith

CHAPTER 44
HOPE, HEALING, AND FAITH

August 15, 2018

Hope, healing, & faith

(In conclusion that is not really a conclusion. The journey continues)

Hope is a universal necessity. We might not think of it, but it really is what gets us through life. Hope is what propels us to get up in the morning. Hope is what motivates us to go to work each day. Hope is what gives us passion and purpose. The necessity of hope crosses all cultural and national boundaries. Without hope, we really have very little, if any, reason to live. Without hope, we live in fear. Sadly, it took the death of my son by suicide from a mental illness to bring me to the awareness of the necessity of hope.

It was my son's death that put me on this journey in search of hope and healing while seeking understanding in the midst of pain. It was my hope that I would gain greater insights on hope and the hope that I and we, in the Church might offer to others. I did some research on the theology of hope. I searched some scriptures and their commentaries on hope. I read a book on someone's personal journey through physical healing of a potentially terminal illness. I have had the gift of time to process, not only to process what I have read, but also to process what I have experienced through the past four years.

I was hoping to discover something concrete …something substantial …something that I and the Church could give to others that they could grab on to and say, "Here, here is the hope that we have to give." What I have come to realize during this time of searching is that I and the Church cannot give hope …at least not a reliable hope. Hope placed in humans and human entities too often disappoints.

We might not be able to give hope, but we still have much hope to offer. We can offer hope by pointing to the God of our hope. We can also offer hope in our support and our care. We can offer hope in welcoming those who are struggling with a mental illness or the loss of a loved one. We can offer hope by offering to walk with them as they continue to seek their healing from mental illness or the pain of grief.

The reason we cannot give hope to someone else is because hope is so personal and individual. Hope is tied to what or to whom we place our faith and trust. Faith and trust are built on personal experiences. Faith and trust are founded and built on a relationship. Relationships and experiences are personal and individual.

I place my hope in the God of creation who was present in the darkness and the chaos. I place my faith in the same God who I have come to know through Jesus Christ. My faith is based on my own personal experiences. My hope is found in the God of my faith. This means that my hope is "*my hope*." I cannot give someone else my hope. My hope is personal and individual. Each person has to find his or her own hope based on who or what this person's faith and trust are placed in.

Other Christians might come to know God through Jesus Christ in a little different way than I do which means their hope in God might be a little different than my hope. People of different religions might come to place their hope in the God that they have come to know through their own personal faith. People who do not believe in a God will have to find their hope in someone or something else. All I can do is share with you the hope that I have in the God of my faith. For me, my hope is in a relationship …my relationship with God.

There is also healing in the relationships. There is healing in placing my hope and my trust in God. There is also healing in my other relationships as well. There is healing through the love and support experienced in community with others. There is healing in hearing the stories of others. There is healing in what might seem to you or to others as simple acts of kindness but are meaningful to the one who is grieving. There is healing in being understood, or at least in someone trying to understand. There is healing in being given the freedom and the space to grieve.

I have also become more aware that there is healing in the journey. There is healing in the process of trying to process through the grief. There is healing in trying to process as to the reason of an untimely death and working through the emotions. There is healing in the searching for understanding of mental illness and suicide. There is healing in seeking answers to why death happens in an unexpected way and at unexpected times. There is healing in the sadness. There is healing in the grieving. There is healing in sharing your story and the story of your loved one. There is healing in sharing time with family. There is healing in new births. There is even healing in going to work each day. There is healing in moving forward with life because you have no other option than to move forward.

Through time and other life experiences, the healing process begins. Slowly, it continues. Through a relationship with God, trust grows. Through that relationship we learn that God has not left us in our pain and grief from the loss of a loved one. God is present in the darkness of mental illness. God is present in the chaos as we attempt to put our lives back together after the death of a loved one.

As for me, the journey continues. I am still in the search for greater understanding of mental illness and suicide. I am still on the journey through grief and pain. Truthfully, I am okay in my brokenness. I am okay in my sadness. I still find and experience much joy even in my sadness. It might sound strange, but for me joy and happiness are not always the opposite of sadness. Many, many times I experience both sadness and happiness at the same time.

Humbly I acknowledge that I do not have great wisdom to share to help ease the pain or assist in the healing from the loss of a loved one. I do not have great knowledge of mental illness or understanding of suicide. But I will continue to work to raise awareness and education on the realities of mental illness and suicide in our communities and in our society. It is indeed with great humility that I share my story and my thoughts with you.

I leave you with this. There is hope in the relationships. There is healing in the journey. It is my hope that maybe through sharing my story of my journey through loss, pain, and grief that you will discover the hope and experience the healing you need for your journey, whatever that might be.

Blessings & peace,
Pastor Keith

Notes

1. "Open My Eyes, That I May See," written by Clara H. Scott. Published 1895

2. Jürgen Moltmann, "Theology of Hope" Abingdon Press, Nashville TN, pg 25.

3. "Life Ain't Always Beautiful," written by Cindi Goodman and Tommy Lee James, Sony/ATV publishing

ABOUT THE AUTHOR

Keith Kraft is the pastor of the United Congregational United Church of Christ in Mobridge South Dakota. Keith is a second career pastor, farming and ranching near Wessington Springs South Dakota until 1997 before entering Eden Seminary in St. Louis. Keith graduated with a Masters of Divinity from Eden Seminary in 2000. After graduation he and his family moved to Mobridge South Dakota where Keith continues to live with his wife Deb. Their youngest son Ben died by suicide December 8, 2014.

36929020R00083

Made in the USA
Columbia, SC
27 November 2018